Aren't You Glad You're Here This Morning?

Thomas E. McGrath

Aren't You Glad You're Here This Morning?
ISBN: Softcover 978-1-951472-59-7
Copyright © 2020 by Thomas E. McGrath

All rights reserved. No part of this book may be reproduced or transmitted in any form or by any means, electronic or mechanical, including photocopying, recording, or by any information storage and retrieval system, without permission in writing from the publisher.

www.parsonsporch.com

Scripture quotations are from the Revised Standard Version of the Bible, copyright 1946, 1952, 1971, 1973, by the Division of Christian Education of the National Council of the Churches of Christ in the U.S.A.

Jamie Nelson provided excellent assistance in the preparation of transcripts.

Cover photo courtesy of Mari McGrath.

Aren't You Glad You're Here This Morning?

Dedication

To my wife Denise and daughter Mari.
Their honesty guides my thought,
Their love guards my heart.

Contents

Dedication ... 3
Introduction ... 9
You're Not One Of Us ... 11
An Act Of God ... 17
Jacob And Esau ... 24
Isaac And Ishmael ... 30
If You Were Shocked Last Sunday That Abraham Gave Away His First-Born Son, Wait Till You Hear Who He Gives Away Today! ... 36
Beth Say A Duh ... 41
What Were They Thinking? ... 48
You Don't See That Every Day! ... 55
The Standard Model, The Higgs Boson (Particle), And The Hadron Collider ... 61
Elizabeth Blackwell And Elizabeth Wiley ... 68
Two Churches, No Post Office, And A New Bridge ... 74
Jesus And The Little Girl ... 81
The Young Man Who Learned To Speak For Himself ... 87
Forgiveness. What It Is And What It Isn't ... 94
In Everything Give Thanks? ... 101
A Doll, A Plastic Cow, And A Painting ... 107
Bermuda Bay ... 113
The Ritual Of Artificial Friendship ... 119
Filioque ... 127
The History Of Halloween ... 133
Walking On Water ... 138
When All The Old Normals Have Changed* ... 144
Christmas Eve ... 151
About the Author ... 153

Introduction

If, as the Apostle Paul told the Athenians, God is not far from any one of us (Acts 17:27), then there must be circumstances, events, or occasions in which God's nearness is especially discernable. The preacher's task includes, at least in part, an effort to rummage through the cascading clutter of the time being to discover and uncover such moments. The greater part of the task is to interpret these moments from the perspective of God's self-disclosure in Jesus of Nazareth. The best, and the hardest, part of the preacher's task is to enable a congregation to embrace these moments with deep reverence and unspeakable joy.

Fred Craddock was a master storyteller. He taught us that what makes a good story good is it's power to awaken in us an appreciation for our own stories. A good story evokes a response of recognition and participation. "Something like that happened to me once. I remember that feeling. That story is my story too." So the sermons I have gathered here, and the stories and events they convey, are offered in the hope that they invite you to celebrate your own stories of occasions of the nearness, perhaps, of God.

The circumstances, events and occasions woven into the fabric of these sermons, if not commonplace, are at least commonly accessible. They are ordinary moments more or less, moments broadly shared. There is a sermon delivered the Sunday before the Olympic Games began, and another for the Sunday before Thanksgiving Day. There is a sermon noting a successful day for the Hadron Collider; another for the Sunday after I painted my front door; yet another for the Sunday after a long-lost Renoir masterpiece was recovered.

Of course there are also sermons occasioned by the familiar celebrations of the church year: Pentecost, All Saints Day, and Christmas Eve. Some of the sermons mark occasions during what the church calendar calls Ordinary Time: Sundays when the Lord's Supper was served; and of course Mother's Day. And in several of the sermons in the collection, the "occasion" is embedded in the Bible story itself:

the day Jesus healed a blind man on the second try; the day estranged brothers met after twenty bitter years apart.

I have gathered these particular sermons because they are each, in some way, tethered to a moment, event, or real-life circumstance. They cover a wide variety of themes. But if there is a common thread running through these pages, it is that God shows up in a lot of places where you wouldn't ordinarily expect God to be, does a lot of things that you might not expect God to do, and loves a lot of people that you might not expect God to love.

The Psalmist declared, "I was glad when they said to me, 'Let us go to the house of the Lord!" (Ps. 122:1) The Gospel *is* good news. "Aren't you glad you're here this morning?" I often asked. As you will see in the pages ahead, I wasn't reluctant to ask folks to follow me into the tall grass or down a rabbit hole. Occasionally folks would greet me after worship confessing, "I didn't know how you would *ever* dig yourself out of that hole." I knew what they were thinking. Their bewildered glances and puzzled expressions told me when to ask. "Aren't you glad you're here this morning?"

The sermons assembled in this volume are presented essentially as they were first delivered. I have resisted the temptation to tidy them up. They are now what they were then: conversational, occasionally awkward, and seasoned with the incidental banter I enjoyed with a congregation whose names I knew, whose Sunday morning faces I cherished, and whose friendship I will ever treasure.

You're Not One Of Us

And Jesus went away from there and withdrew to the district of Tyre and Sidon. And behold a Canaanite woman from that region came out and cried, "Have mercy on me, O Lord, Son of David: my daughter is severely possessed by a demon." But he did not answer her a word. And his disciples came and begged him saying, "Send her away for she is crying after us." He answered, "I was sent only to the lost sheep of the house of Israel." But she came and knelt before him, saying "Lord, help me." And he answered, "It is not fair to take the children's bread and throw it to the dogs." She said, "Yes Lord, but even the dogs eat the crumbs that fall from the master's table." And Jesus answered her, "O woman, great is your faith! Be it done for you as you desire." And her daughter was healed instantly. Matthew 15:21-28

You probably know more about judging dog shows than I do. I guarantee you this: there are very few people who know less about judging dog shows than I do. I've never understood how you choose the best among all those beautiful dogs, all perfectly groomed, all well trained. How do you choose between them?

At the Westminster Kennel Club Dog Show they judge dogs in seven categories. Who knows the seven categories? Impress us. Someone stand up and recite the seven categories. Anyone? Anyone? Alright. Hound, Sporting, Working, Herding, Toy, Terrier, and Non-Sporting. So take the Hound category, for example. In the Hound category you might have a Basset Hound, a Bloodhound, a Wolfhound, and a Greyhound, among others. Now think about how different each of those dogs is from the others. Basset Hounds are just adorable. Bloodhounds are kind of goofy looking. The Wolfhound is tall and handsome in a shaggy kind of way. The Greyhound is sleek and regal. How do you pick? How do you decide the best dog in the category? Is the Basset Hound a more perfect Basset than the Bloodhound is a perfect Bloodhound? What's the criteria? And then in the final round the winner in each of the seven categories compete for Best of Show. So in the final round you're comparing seven very different dogs. So is the Sporting dog a more perfect Sporting dog than the Herding dog is a perfect Herding dog? Is the Working dog a more perfect Working Dog than the Non-Sporting dog is a perfect Non-Sporting dog? Should I go on, or do you see the dilemma?

The favorite going in this year was a Wire-Haired Pointer named Oakley. Oakley had won eighty-two first place ribbons. But the winner, as you may know, was Banana Joe, an Affenpinscher. Banana Joe would have been considered the dark-horse contender (or the dark-dog entry). How's your German? Do you know what *Affenpinscher* means? *Afffen* means monkey. Banana Joe is a Monkey Dog. If you looked closely at the face of an Affenpinscher, you would see the resemblance to a monkey; hence, the name for this champion, *Banana Joe*. And Joe is the first Affenpinscher ever to win Best of Show at Westminster. Never happened before.

So this year, at least, Banana Joe is a more perfect Toy Dog than Oakley is a perfect Sporting Dog.

I know what you're thinking by now: where is he going with this? Stay with me.

We live in a world that loves categories. Black, White. Rich, Poor. Red, Blue. Gay, Straight. Boomer, Millennial, Gen-X. And the Church has categories too. Believer, Unbeliever. Saved, Unsaved. Protestant, Catholic. Member, Non-member. (Immediately following this service, we have a congregational meeting. I don't want any of you non-members hiding in the restroom during the Benediction, then sneaking back in here to miss lunch like the rest of us, just to linger over every word of this fascinating Annual Report.)

Categories. The thing about categories is that they inevitably offer us the temptation to say to someone, "You're not one of us."

And that's exactly what the disciples of Jesus said to the poor woman in our story today, "You are not one of us. Go away." She was a Canaanite or, more precisely, a Syro-Phoenician. Remember the Phoenicians from your high school history class? They were the world's first sailors, sea-going traders whose purple cloth and exquisite glassware were in demand everywhere fine products were sold. She was not a Jew like the disciples. She was Syro-Phoenician.

And before we even get into the juicy parts of the story, there are two absurd realities right here. First, Jesus and his disciples are in *her* space. They have crossed the fence into her yard, the region of Tyre and Sidon. And even in *her* native land they apparently think they are superior to her!

The second irony is this: the Phoenicians had settled Palestine more than 500 years before Abraham and his clan had even arrived! And the Phoenicians *helped* the Jews! (Read about this for yourself in II Samuel 5 and I Kings 5.) Hiram, King of Tyre, helped David build his house. Then Hiram provided to David's son Solomon the carpenters, craftsmen, and raw materials to build that fabulous Temple! Remember the cedars of Lebanon? From Hiram. Then Hiram helped Solomon build a navy!

Jesus surely knew all of this history. So what's going on here?

Please notice how carefully Matthew sets this up. She is a Canaanite (not a Jew). She is an interruption (Jesus has come here to get some time away from the crowds back home). She is a woman (shouldn't be addressing a man in public). And she wants help for a daughter (not a son). The odds are stacked against her. But we all know that our Jesus will come to her rescue. Right? We're expecting a Hallmark Moment here, aren't we?

When she first asks his help, Jesus doesn't even answer her. When she kneels at his feet and pleads, "Lord, help me," he insults her! "It's not right to take the children's bread and throw it to the dogs." He calls her a dog! It's bad enough to utter a slur behind someone's back. But to insult her to her face? It must have happened this way, because you wouldn't make up a story like this and put it in our Bible. How do you explain this?

Some commentators explain this by saying that Jesus is *testing* her. No. It is a test, but not of her. Jesus is testing his disciples! He gives voice to an ugly prejudice common in that day. This is what the disciples were thinking about her: she's not one of us. So Jesus lets them hear for themselves how ugly it is. And this is the test: will any one of them object? Will even one have the decency or courage to say, "Lord, this isn't right; she may not be one of us, but she is a human being; she is asking for our help for her beloved child; she has humbled herself. What you just said to her is offensive and it is wrong. We need to help her." Will anyone speak on her behalf? Would I have spoken up? Would you have? And from the clowns he is counting on to help him save the world, only silence.

But the woman is not silent. Her response to this insult, under other circumstances, might seem almost charming. "Yes Lord," she said, "yet even the dogs eat the crumbs that fall from their master's table." Anyone who has ever owned a dog understands this. Can't you see Oakley or Banana Joe under the table impatiently waiting for crumbs or mashed potatoes or whatever you feed your dog from the table?

She stands her ground. She absorbs the insult and presses on for her daughter's sake. She fights back. This is an amazing story! She refuses to be defined by what other people think of her. (I worked a long time on that sentence, so remember it.) She won't be confined by a category that diminishes her. "I may not be just like you," she is saying, "but I am a person. And my daughter is a person. And I believe that God's love is for us too!" She believes that God has drawn a circle that includes a Canaanite woman and her daughter. And Jesus agrees.

"O woman, great is your faith," he answers. That's what faith is. Faith is believing that God's love includes you. "Be it done for you as you desire," he said. And her daughter was instantly healed.

How does it feel to be the "problem"? That's how the disciples saw her, as the problem. An interruption. An irritation. But she defined herself as a child of God. And Jesus praised her for her faith.

I have one more story to tell you. Then we're done.

Virgil Cruz was African American. He was also my Professor of New Testament Studies at Dubuque Seminary. He was highly esteemed and an excellent teacher. He was one of the reasons I enrolled at Dubuque.

Aren't You Glad You're Here This Morning?

Dr. Cruz did his doctoral work at the Free University of Amsterdam. While he was in Holland, he fell in love with a Dutch girl. And she fell in love with him. And she was White. Eventually the day arrived for them to ask her parents for their blessing. They had dinner, then adjourned to the parlor for coffee and the conversation. Her parents weren't dumb; they had seen the obvious affection. They knew what was coming.

Virgil had rehearsed his speech. "We love one another, etc., etc., and we hope you will give us your blessing." Her father had rehearsed his speech too. (You understand of course that I wasn't actually there. As the events of that evening were described to me, this is more or less the way it went.) Her father said that they loved their daughter and trusted her judgment. They believed Virgil to be a good man and wanted to bless their plans to marry. But they did have one concern, not an objection exactly, but a concern.

Well Virgil was ready for that and launched into his prepared remarks about the special challenges facing interracial couples, and how these challenges might actually strengthen their …. But her father interrupted Virgil, waved him off before he could get it all out. "Virgil," he said quite firmly, "We have no concern about that whatsoever."

Virgil recalculated. "Well maybe you're concerned about the religious differences. I'm Presbyterian; you folks are Dutch Reformed. Is that your concern?"

"Virgil, we have no concern about that whatsoever."

So then Virgil said, "Well I hope to become a professor. Maybe you hoped that your daughter would marry someone destined for a more prestigious calling, Law or Medicine perhaps."

Her father replied, "Virgil, teaching is a profession we honor and admire. We have no concern about that whatsoever."

Virgil was stumped now. "What is it then? What is your concern?"

Her father hesitated. "It's not easy to talk about, Virgil, and we hope you won't be offended. We think you are an honorable man. And our daughter loves you and we love you. Our only concern is this: you are an American."

I'll bet you didn't see that coming. Categories! The world loves categories. The world is always prepared to say, "You're not one of us. You don't belong." But faith says, "You belong!" Jesus says, "You belong." We all belong. We belong to a loving God.

Let us pray.

Loving God, break down the categories that keep us apart. In Jesus Christ, Amen.

An Act Of God

You have heard that it was said, "You shall love your neighbor and hate your enemy." But I say to you, Love your enemies, and pray for those who persecute you so that you may be sons of your Father who is in heaven. For he makes his sun to rise on the evil and on the good and sends rain on the just and on the unjust. For if you love those who love you, what reward have you? Do not even the tax collectors do the same? And if you salute only your brothers and sisters, what more are you doing than others? Do not even the Gentiles do the same? You therefore must be perfect as your heavenly Father is perfect. Matthew 5:43-48

The following is an actual Associated Press dispatch from a few years' ago. It comes from the nation of South Africa:

Lay Preacher Gert Easel, Chairman of South Africa's Anti-Miniskirt League, has prophesied doom and divine wrath ever since the local girls began to wear their hemlines shorter. When Western Cape Province was rocked by an earthquake, which killed nine people and caused millions of dollars of damage, Easel immediately issued a statement blaming miniskirts for the disaster.

Are natural disasters the acts of God? Does God single out families, communities, nations for particular acts of vengeance and wrath? Is an earthquake an act of God? Is a flood? Is a hurricane an act of God? A wildfire? How about cancer? How about an automobile accident? How about a fall? Are these acts of God?

I intend to do the best I can to give you my own answer to that before we go today. But before we do that, I want to issue a word of caution for all of us. We really ought to approach these questions with a good deal of humility. There's a lot about God that I don't understand. It seems to me that it's arrogant, foolishly arrogant, for anyone to try to say with certainty which events are God's doing, and which events are not. So will you join me in a spirit of humility as we seek to work our way through this question?

The problem for us as Christian believers today is that when we turn to our Bibles, and especially when we turn to the Old Testament, we find story after story in which natural disasters are reported to be the direct acts of God. Earthquakes, volcanic eruptions, hailstorms, famines, droughts – these are all in one place or another attributed to God's direct action intended as punishment. You only have to turn to the first book of the Bible, Genesis, and a few chapters in you've got Noah and the flood. God flooded the earth because he was disappointed in his creation and wished to punish it. A few chapters later, God sends plagues on the Egyptians who refuse to let his people go. A few chapters after that, we find Joshua leading the armies of Israel against their foes the Amorites. And I don't understand the astronomy of this, but the text says God made the sun stand still to prolong the day so that Joshua's troops could continue to slaughter the Amorites right down to the very last man. God is reported to have done that.

Now there's no doubt that Noah and Joshua and the others *believed* that God was directly acting. But they believed many things that we don't believe anymore. Now I want to be very careful about how I say that. I'm not saying anything controversial here, nothing radical or new. This is something we all know once we stop and think about it. There are lots of things that they believed that we don't believe anymore. They believed in human slavery. The Old Testament clearly approved of human slavery. We don't believe in that anymore. The Bible clearly approved of polygamy, multiple marriages. Many of the Old Testament heroes that we revere had more than one wife. Solomon, reported to have been the wisest man in the world, had many, many wives. Go figure.

We don't believe that anymore. We've changed our mind about that. The central act in Hebrew worship was animal sacrifice. If I brought a little lamb into this sanctuary this morning and did to that little lamb what they regularly did to their little lambs, women would run screaming out the door and parents would never bring their children to this church again. And I would in all likelihood be arrested and spend some time in jail. We don't do that anymore. They did the things they did not because they were inherently cruel or wicked but because they operated in a different *belief system* than we do. They did what they did because they believed what they believed, but we no longer live under that belief system.

And it seems to me that the question of whether God causes natural disasters may be in that category of things that they believed that we have come to have a different understanding of. Because now we operate not in the Old Testament exclusively but in the New Testament. And new means new. It is a different perspective. When Jesus comes, things change. The way we *think* about things has changed. "Be not conformed to this world, but be transformed by the renewal of your *mind*," St. Paul admonished. This is what Paul was talking about. Exactly what we are talking about this morning. When Jesus comes, things do change. When I stand at the communion table and we serve the sacrament of the Lord's Supper, what do I say? What does the pastor say when the cup is lifted? "Behold, this cup is the new covenant." It's new. There's something *new* in the message of Jesus that requires us to change our old ways of thinking. This is why the early church, the early Christians who were themselves Jews, were quickly expelled from the synagogues. Because it was clear to everybody that there was something new going on.

We have the advantage of hearing an opinion from Jesus Christ himself about this question of natural disasters and God's involvement in them. You can look it up yourself, Luke 13:3. You can check me out this afternoon and make sure I'm getting it right. Luke 13:3 is a paragraph, a chapter, we pay far too little attention to, in my opinion. In that chapter, some folks come to Jesus and report to him what they've just seen on CNN, a terrible event. Pilate's soldiers have murdered a lot of innocent people down at the temple. "Jesus, have you heard about this? What do you say about this?"

So Jesus asked, "Do you think that these people who were murdered down at the temple were worse sinners than everybody else? Do you think," he asked his questioners, "that's why they died? Because God was punishing them?" Then Jesus answered his own question. He said, "No." He said it that clearly: No. And then he added his own example, which must have been from the news that had only recently happened, because it's very precise. He said, "And what about the time when the tower of Siloam collapsed on 18 people?" The numbers are exact; it must have been in everybody's mind. Jesus said, "What about the tower falling down and killing 18 people?" (Must have been a little earthquake.) Jesus said, "Do you think those 18 people were worse sinners than everybody else?" And he answered his own question again. He said "No." That's not how God works. These events, human violence, and a natural disaster, are not the direct acts of God. They're not God's judgment on particular people or particular families or particular nations.

Now Jesus did go on to say, "There will be a day of judgment, but it comes for all of us together at the end of time." I believe in a day of judgment. I'm a husband. I know that when you've done something that you shouldn't have done, or when you haven't done something that you were supposed to do, there will one day come a day when it all comes out.

But the message of Jesus Christ is that the day of judgment will be a day of mercy and forgiveness because of what Jesus has done. It will be a day of reconciliation and joyful celebration as the Lamb of God takes away the sins of the world and we are reunited with God. Jesus taught that God wears the face toward us of love. Not of wrath, not of vengeance, but of love. God so loved the world, we say, that he gave his only son. This is what is new. This is the new understanding of God's heart and God's work.

Now, that brings us finally to our scripture text for today. How much more clearly could Jesus say it? The sun shines on the good and the evil alike. The rain falls on the just and the unjust. In this world, in this time, bad things happen to bad people, but bad things happen to good people too. They are not God's direct acts of judgment. Rain falls if you're under a cloud. If you're under a cloud, it's not a sign that God hates you, that God is judging you, it's just a sign that there's too much moisture in the air. It's a natural process. That's what I think Jesus is teaching. The rain, the sun, even a hurricane, even an earthquake, comes as a consequence as a sequence of natural processes, natural laws that God has built into the fabric of his universe. They are not direct acts of vengeance. That's how I see it. That's how I understand what Jesus himself said.

Finally, I saw a photograph this week. Just a fleeting glimpse of a photograph, and I didn't catch all the details. Maybe you saw it? And it had a caption imprinted across the photograph. And this is what it showed, so far as I can recall: In the background there was a devastated village. It wasn't clear what had happened but the village was clearly in ruins and there were people standing in front of the village milling about, kind of helpless looking. And there was a road in the foreground of the picture, a road leading down toward the village. But that wasn't the focus of the picture. Not the road and not the village. The focus of the picture was a man. We only saw his back because he was walking down the road toward the village. It seemed to me that he might have been wearing camouflage fatigues but I couldn't tell that for sure. Might have been a doctor's coat that he was wearing. I couldn't tell that for sure. But I did see that he was balancing a large carton on his shoulder. And emblazoned on that carton was a red cross. And that was the focus of that picture. And the caption read simply, "An Act of God."

Not the devastation, but the compassion. God is present wherever people suffer but not as the cause of the suffering. God is present in the hearts and hands, in the tears and the tenderness of those who have come to help.

And that reminds me of Bill. Do you have time? Bill was an elder in the first church I served. Every Sunday Bill sat in the front row nearest our wonderful organist, who happened to be his wife. I've served with many elders who were reflexively skeptical of the Pastor's new ideas, especially if they involved the expenditure of church funds. But that was not Bill. Bill's attitude was, "If our Pastor thinks this is what we need to do, let's try it. We can do this." I liked Bill. A lot.

Bill learned that his neighbors' twelve-year-old daughter needed surgery for a heart defect. But the hospital required a large down payment in advance, much more than her parents could afford. So after a few phone calls a benefit auction was planned, to be held in the Springfield Township Volunteer Fire Station. In the meantime donations of items to sell at the auction were gathered from the community. But ours was not a wealthy community, so many of the donated items were of dubious market value. And that's where the auctioneer started.

Bill was seated in the front row. The first lot to be auctioned consisted of two plastic Frisbees. Nobody bid. Then Bill raised his hand and the auctioneer shouted, "Sold!" Then there was a well-used galvanized bucket. Bill was the only bidder. Soon he added a rusty child's bicycle to his growing pile of what was essentially junk. I leaned over to my wife and whispered, "What does Bill want with all that stuff?" I wasn't as smart then as I am now, so it took me a while to figure it out. Bill was in his own way reminding us all why we were there that night. Soon the bidding grew absurdly competitive. A good sum of money was raised; the surgery was completely successful.

That night at the Springfield Township Volunteer Fire Station has stayed with me all these years because of what I learned a few months later. Bill was a truck driver, but he also had a small farm where he raised pigs. As it was told to me, a few years earlier Bill was awakened one night by an ominous orange glow outside the bedroom window. He threw on some clothes and hurried outside, but he could see it was too late. The barn where he kept the pigs was engulfed in flames. Despite the horrifying sight and sounds of the burning barn, there was nothing he could do. But that was not the worst of it. The wind was blowing hard that night, and it was blowing straight toward his house. There were already glowing embers on his roof. Bill threw a ladder against the side of his house, grabbed the garden hose, and climbed as high as he could to fend off the flames.

Then he heard the sirens. The very welcome sirens. Before the trucks even came to a full stop in his front yard, the volunteer firefighters of Springfield Township had leapt from running boards and were working the hoses. They saved his house. But by the time they got Bill down from the ladder, his shirt was scorched by the sparks and his back blistered by the heat.

There was some suspicion of arson. There were rumors of shadowy figures disappearing into the woods about the time the fire started. Bill might have been bitter. But he wasn't. He might have held a grudge. But he didn't. He might even have blamed God. But instead, he continued to be what he always had been: a good neighbor.

Aren't You Glad You're Here This Morning?

That's the reason that what happened in the Springfield Township Volunteer Fire Station that evening was no surprise. A young woman and her parents needed help. And Bill was in the front row.

That's what an act of God looks like.

Let us pray:

Loving God, enable us again and again to entrust ourselves to one another and to you. In Jesus Christ, Amen.

Jacob And Esau

The same night he arose and took his two wives, and his two maids, and his eleven children, and crossed the ford of the Jabbok. He took them and sent them across the stream, and likewise everything that he had. And Jacob was left alone; and a man wrestled with him until the breaking of the day. When the man saw that he did not prevail against Jacob, he touched the hollow of his thigh; and Jacob's thigh was put out of joint as he wrestled with him. The he said, "Let me go, for the day is breaking." But Jacob said, "I will not let you go unless you bless me." And he said to him, "What is your name?" And he said," Jacob." Then he said, "Your name shall no more be called Jacob, but Israel, for you have striven with God and with men, and have prevailed." Then Jacob asked him, "Tell me, I pray, your name." But he said, "Why is it that you ask my name?" And there he blessed him. So Jacob called the name of the place Peniel, saying, "For I have seen God face to face, and yet my life is preserved." Genesis 32:22-30

This is a complicated story. And it may be that the best we can do with this story is to get this: God can still use a crooked stick to draw a straight line. If you get nothing else from this story – and you may not – get that. God can use a crooked stick to draw a straight line.

Jacob is a crooked stick! But God used Jacob to draw a straight line down through the generations, about forty generations in all, from Jacob's life to another Jacob, who was the father of a man named Joseph, who was the father of Jesus! God can draw a straight line. And that may be the best we can do with this story.

But there is much more to the story than that, because the story of Jacob includes the story of a brother, his twin brother Esau. The Bible very often uses the relationships of brothers as a window through which God's truth may shine. The Bible's first brothers were Cain and Abel. Cain got jealous and murdered Abel. And that story becomes a window through which we view the tragic violence, which has been so much a part of the history of humankind. Or, the best example is probably Jesus' parable of the Prodigal Son, whose older brother resents his restoration to the family. Jesus would surely have known the story of Jacob and Esau and, I believe, adapted it for his parable of the prodigal.

People who belong together sometimes get separated. Like brothers, people who belong together sometimes find themselves painfully distant from one another. It happens in families. It happens in neighborhoods. It happens in nations. People who share the same heritage and history are sometimes separated by the controversies of the moment: red states, blue states, liberals, conservatives. Believe it or not, it can even happen in churches! Maybe this story can open a window for us.

Jacob had two life-altering encounters with God. Now we've talked before about the first encounter. Humor me and nod your head that you remember the account of Jacob's vision of a ladder extending into heaven, angels ascending and descending, and God's promise to bless Jacob. Remember? Do you want me to go over it again? No? Okay. Well, that encounter occurred as Jacob was *fleeing* Esau after scamming him out of his birthright. He is running in fear for his life on account of Esau's angry vow of revenge. And he has this vision of a ladder. You might even call him a ladder day saint. And that's the setting for Jacob's first encounter with God.

So here is Jacob: grasping, scheming, cunning, calculating, and on the run. Into a far country he goes. And the first thing that happens is that he stops for a drink at the well and meets a young woman. And falls head-over-heels in love. Rachel is her name. Marriage negotiations ensue. Laban, her father, says, "She's a pretty special girl; if you want to marry Rachel you will have to work for me seven years for the privilege of her hand." "Deal," Jacob answers. He's really smitten.

Seven years pass. At last, the wedding day! Down the aisle she comes; the minister says the words (that's not exactly how it happened, but you get the picture). Jacob lifts the veil to kiss his bride. And it's not Rachel! (You know this story, don't you?) It's Leah, Rachel's *older* sister! What's this? He goes to his new father-in-law Laban for an explanation. "Oh, I thought you understood our customs," Laban replies. "In our culture the oldest sister must be married before a younger sister; if you want to marry Rachel, you'll have to work another seven years." Well Jacob had not understood that! By the way, the Bible describes Rachel as fair and beautiful, while Leah is described as poor of eyesight, which some translators have interpreted to mean that she wasn't much to look at.

So Jacob the scammer has been scammed! The schemer has just been schemed. He's in love, so he signs up for another seven. But he's not going to take this lying down, as they say. He comes up with a plan. (I love these stories; do you have time for this, because it's going to take a little while?) Jacob, still fuming at having been taken by Laban, goes to his father-in- law with something like this: "Dad, some day I will be taking your two daughters and going off on my own. Not right away, but some day I will need to provide for them, and for your grandchildren. Wouldn't it be good if I had a little nest-egg started so I could keep them in the comfort to which they are accustomed?" So Laban said, "What do you have in mind?"

"Well, I don't want much," Jacob said. Gesturing out toward a field white with flocks of sheep and goats, he continued his pitch. "I would be quite satisfied if you gave me only the few spotted sheep, we see out there. And I would need goats; would you cede me only those few goats that have stripes?" That's all he asked for, the spotted and the striped. Laban took a quick formal inventory of his flocks. Here and there, maybe one in a hundred, was a sheep with a little black spot on its ear or under its chin. And here and there among the hundreds of goats were a few odd goats with brown stripes. "Deal," he said.

What Laban failed to consider was that Jacob was the foreman of the animal husbandry department. As the years pass, Jacob runs a version of E-Harmony dating service for sheep and goats. He cleverly insists that the male sheep with spots date only the female sheep that are white. Likewise, he arranges that the male goats that are striped date only the female goats that have no stripes. So by the time Jacob is ready to strike out on his own, most of Laban's sheep are spotted, and most of his goats are striped. And now they belong to Jacob! The schemer has his revenge.

Well, that goes on for twenty years. Jacob is away from the homeland he fled all those years ago. And then there was a stirring in his heart.

Twenty years before, on the night of that vision of the ladder, God had promised Jacob that one-day he could return to the land of his birth. And now, having cherished the hope of home for so long, he gathers up his two wives and their children, his two slave girls and their children, and his now huge flocks of spotted sheep and striped goats, and everything else he has accumulated. He forms up his caravan and sets his sights for home. Jacob and his caravan prepare to cross the Jabbok, not to flee as twenty years before, but to return.

Then Jacob gets the worst possible news: "Esau is on his way to meet you, Jacob. He knows you're coming, and he has a little welcoming party planned. And for the celebration, he's bringing along 400 heavily armed friends to help welcome you home."

And this is how it goes. Jacob the schemer calculates what it will take to buy off his brother Esau's anger. He decides to give Esau 220 goats, 220 sheep, 30 camels and their colts, 40 cows, 10 bulls, and 30 asses. He sent them on ahead as a gift. (You can read all of this yourself in the verses immediately preceding today's scripture lesson.) That's Plan A.

But Jacob has a Plan B. Plan A may not work. Esau in his anger may just gobble up this extravagant gift and keep on coming. What then? So now. Jacob divides up his family and sends them out to the front of the caravan. Slave girls and their children are the front line; they're the cannon fodder. Leah and her children are next, in the second row. Rachel, whom he loves, and her son Joseph are the rear guard. If Esau's anger is not satisfied by the gift of livestock, and he attacks the caravan, he can hack his way through the slave girls and their children. And if he still isn't satisfied, he can hack away at Leah's family. And hopefully Esau and his men will get tired hacking before they get to Rachel, Joseph, and Jacob. That's Plan B.

So Jacob sends them all across the Jabbok into Esau's path. He remains behind, alone. And this is the moment in which he has his second encounter with God. Now from the text, we don't know exactly what to call this. Is it a vision? Is it a dream? As he sleeps, he is awakened with the sensation of cold hands upon him, which he must surely have assumed to be Esau. But it's not Esau. Is it a man? Is it an angel? And there in the darkness, they're wrestling!

And what the "wrestling" means is more or less up to you because the Bible doesn't say exactly. Is Jacob wrestling with his own guilty conscience about how he's treated people, especially his brother? Is he wrestling with his fear? Is he wrestling with God? Maybe your experiences of "wrestling" with something or someone will shape what you make of Jacob's wrestling.

But this much we know: the wrestling changes him. He is given a new name, *Israel*, meaning, "You have striven with God and with men and have prevailed." And he has a limp now, which means that the wrestling has wounded him in some way, made him perhaps more vulnerable, less proudly self-sufficient. He is changed; and we hope he is changed for the better!

And so at last we are almost to the end of our story. The sun rises. The angel, if it was an angel, is gone. Jacob crosses the river. Jacob walks right on past Rachel and Joseph. Jacob walks right on past Leah and her kids. He walks right on past the slave girls and their kids. He walks right on past the gift of grazing goats and sheep and camels and cows and bulls and asses. Jacob walks to the front of the caravan, then beyond, on his way alone, to face his brother Esau. At last, Jacob will be a man! Jacob will take whatever Esau intends to serve up to him. He has mustered his courage, no more hiding behind his family, no more running away. He's going to face it, whatever comes. But *what* comes he could not ever have foreseen.

Jacob lifted up his eyes and, behold, Esau was coming. Jacob bows himself to the ground. Esau is still coming. Jacob bows again. And again. Seven times, until he draws near to his brother. But Esau runs to meet him. Esau embraces his brother Jacob, kisses his face, his beard, his neck. Locked in one another's arms, both men weep. "To see your face," Jacob says to Esau, "is like seeing the face of God, with such favor you have received me!" Two people who belonged together are together again at last.

And a couple of chapters later in their story, their father Isaac dies. "Isaac breathed his last; and he died and was gathered to his people, old and full of days; and his sons *Esau and Jacob* buried him." (Gen.35:29) Esau and Jacob, together.

Now we all know that Jacob is a towering figure in the Biblical story. An entire nation bears his new name, Israel. Jacob gets the headlines. But behind the front page, there is a quiet hero here. Esau. He makes it all possible. His grace toward his brother makes peaceful reunion possible. When Jacob said that seeing Esau's face was like seeing the face of God, he was saying more than he knew.

Esau is the quiet hero who, though he had been wounded by his brother years before, nevertheless holds the world together. He holds the world together for love's sake. The world is full of Jacobs. It's more of Esau that we need.

Perhaps today Esau is who you will be. Let us pray.

Lord, we thank you for ever working to bring us together in love. In Jesus Christ, Amen.

Isaac And Ishmael

And the child grew and was weaned. Abraham made a great feast on the day that Isaac was weaned; but Sarah saw the son of Hagar the Egyptian whom she had born to Abraham playing with her son Isaac. So she said to Abraham, "Cast out this slave woman with her son. For the son of this slave woman shall not be heir with my son Isaac." And the thing was very displeasing to Abraham on account of his son. But God said to Abraham, "Be not displeased because of the lad, because of your slave woman. Whatever Sarah says to you, do as she tells you. For through Isaac shall your descendants be named. And I will make a nation of the son of the slave woman also, because he is your offspring."

So Abraham rose early in the morning and took bread and a skin of water and gave it to Hagar, putting it on her shoulder along with the child, and sent her away. And she departed and wandered in the wilderness of Beersheba. When the water in the skin was gone, she placed the child under one of the bushes and then she went and sat down over against him a good way off, for she said," Let me not look upon the death of my child." But as she sat over against him, the child lifted up his voice and wept. And God heard the voice of the lad. And the angel of God called to Hagar from heaven and said to her, "What troubles you Hagar? Fear not, for God has heard the voice of the child where he is." Genesis 21: 8-17

Abraham. Isaac. Jacob. You got it? The three generations with which the Hebrew people began. Abraham. Isaac. Jacob. God promised Abraham that he would be the father of two great peoples. Through his son Isaac, Abraham became the father of the Hebrew people. They gave us, gave the world, the faith of Judaism, the Old Testament, the Ten Commandments, the Psalms, Moses, David, Isaiah, Jeremiah, all of that. The children of Isaac, the Hebrew people, have given the world great contributions in art and literature and science and medicine. God promised that Isaac would be the father of a great people, and he is the father of a great people.
But God also promised that Ishmael, the other boy, would be the father of a great people. Ishmael grew up on the Arabian Peninsula.

And so by history and by tradition, Ishmael has become the father of the Arab peoples of the world. And through the Arab peoples, we have great gifts of art and literature and science. We have those marvelous stories of Aladdin's lamp, Scheherazade, Sinbad the Sailor. Ishmael's descendants invented the first calculator of sorts. You remember it from your high school days, that little machine with the beads? The abacus. The abacus, a contribution of the Arab mathematicians. They created the concept of zero, which is, after all, with the number one, the basis upon which all modern computing takes place. Zero and one. I don't understand that, but I'm told that's how it works. So you could even argue that the Arab peoples have given the world gifts, which have led to Google and the internet and all of that.

And the Arab peoples have also given the world a great faith, the faith of Islam. Like Judaism, Islam is a faith that worships one God, has a strong moral code, an emphasis on what is right and wrong. Sadly, many today form attitudes and opinions about the Muslim faith based on a tiny, tiny minority of violent extreme people. They no more represent Islam than the Ku Klux Klan represents Christianity.

So the world has received marvelous gifts through the children of Isaac and also through the children of Ishmael, just as God promised. But lots of people are surprised to remember that Ishmael was *first*. Ishmael was the first son. And I am sure you understand how important it was to be the first son.

Ishmael was the first son. And this is how it happened. You know this story. Abraham and Sarah were married many, many, many years. Grew into old age, no children. Finally Sarah got impatient. She had this Egyptian slave girl, Hagar, so she gave Hagar to her husband. And pretty soon Hagar is with child and gives birth to Ishmael.

What shall we say to this? This is terrible! If wrong is wrong and always has been wrong and always will be wrong, this is wrong. Hagar is a slave. That's wrong.
And Sarah gives her like a piece of property to her husband to make babies with. This is wrong. If you did this, you'd be in jail! Now I don't mean that we have to judge all of these Old Testament characters and all of these Old Testament stories by our modern standards of culture

and morality. But this is wrong! This is not a good way for people to treat people. But this is how the story goes.

And the redeeming part of the story is that Abraham the father loves his son Ishmael. He just loves him. I could say he loves him like his own son, but he is his own son! He loves him. And you can see Abraham in his old age with this little lad. They are more like a grandfather and a grandson than a father and a son. I imagine Abraham taking him out to the pasture, showing him how to call the sheep, taking him fishing if they went fishing in those days, teaching him all the things that a father or a grandfather wants to pass on to his beloved child. They're inseparable. First, in the early years, Abraham helping the little boy Ishmael; now, in the later years as Ishmael grows stronger and taller, now it's Ishmael helping Abraham across the stream or up the hill. They were inseparable.

And then the unexpected happens. Sarah is with child. And Sarah gives birth to a child of her own, Isaac. The second -- second! -- son of Abraham. Things go along fine for a while. Now Ishmael has a pal, a brother. You can see them there. There may have been eight- or ten-years' difference in their age; it's hard to tell from the narrative. Ishmael the older boy, taking his younger brother, you know, out to the ball game, teaching him how to throw stones with a sling, teaching him how to talk to girls, you know? Brothers! They were brothers together in that household.

And then one day Sarah looks out the window and sees Ishmael, Hagar's son, and Isaac, her son, playing together. And she realizes that her son Isaac will never be at the top. He's the second. And she gets jealous. And this begins to eat at her. And it becomes an obsession. Finally she goes to her husband Abraham; and the narrator is so very careful in how he tells this story. Sarah will not even say their names. Will not even pronounce the name of the maid, the slave that she gave to her husband those years ago. Will not even say the name of the boy who now befriends her son Isaac. She says, "That son of that slave woman and the slave woman herself, send them away."

And Abraham's heart is broken because he loves them both. They're both his sons and he loves them both. So he asks God what to do.

And the answer in verse 12 is probably, at least for us who are married men, the most difficult verse in all of the Bible. You think the Ten Commandments are hard? Read verse 12 of chapter 21, where Abraham believes that God has said to him, "Do whatever your wife tells you to do." That's the 11th Commandment!

Now, you may suppose that because Abraham was an old man, he forgot to put in his hearing aids that day and that what God really said was *don't* do what your wife tells you to do. You can work on that angle if you want. But I think God is more subtle than that. I think there is another answer. When God said to Abraham, "Do whatever your wife tells you to do," Abraham, if he had been paying attention, might have answered, "Which wife?" Because by all the laws of decency, Hagar is as much a wife to him as Sarah is. I think God asks the question in a way that points out to Abraham what a mess he's gotten himself into here. Which "wife" is he going to obey?

But he sides with Sarah. He sends them away. With a sack of bread and a couple of bottles of water, down the road they go. The road leads out into the desert. Does Abraham know this is a death sentence? He surely must know.

You want to ask, "What's wrong with you people? How could you do something like this?" And in fact, there are more than a few stories in the Bible in which that is our natural first reaction. How can this be? This is a terrible story and I sometimes think that because this is so hard to sort out, maybe we preachers haven't done a very good job in addressing the problems in such stories. Some stories in the Bible we read for the good examples that they show. And they're in our Bible so that when we read them, we're inspired to imitate the courage and the justice and the goodness we find in those stories. "This is how God wants us to live," we say when we read those stories.

But there are these other stories in the Bible in which I think just the opposite is true. And sometimes they're presented in a very subtle way, but God must surely want us, when we read this story to say, "No! No, that's not the way to live, that's not the way God wants us to be. That cannot be what a loving God intends!" And very often these stories are presented to us with no alternative but for the reader to decide how to respond.

Here is what I think is happening in this story. It's not that Abraham is such a bad person; it's not that Sarah is such a bad person. They are both caught in a system that they cannot imagine a way out of. What we have in this story, I think, is a failure of imagination. In their culture, what they do makes a certain kind of sense. In their culture, there are masters and therefore there must be slaves. In their culture, there are first sons who get most everything and therefore there must be second sons who don't get very much. In their culture, if Isaac is to go up, Ishmael must come down. And they cannot imagine another way to be together as people. This happens. This happens to people, this happens to families. They get stuck and can't imagine another way, an alternative to how they have always been. It happens to nations. It even happens to churches and congregations. You've been doing the same thing; you get so comfortable with something that it's hard to image doing it any other way.

But God is not bound! God is not trapped by the limitations of our imaginations! God is always pushing us out to new opportunities to love this broken world back together.

When the child and his mother, Ishmael and Hagar, are perishing there in the desert, God hears their cry. God intervenes to keep the promise, to rescue the child and his mother. *God hears Ishmael's cry.*

There is a postscript, which gives the story a more or less a happy ending. If you read at the end of the story of Abraham, the narrator says, "So Abraham was laid to rest in a good old age, an old man full of years, gathered to his people. Isaac and Ishmael, his sons, buried him." So whatever happened in the intervening years, the brothers eventually came together again to bury the father who loved them both.

But don't be in too big of a hurry to put a happy ending on this story. There is sadness here. Remember that awful day when Abraham closed the gate behind his first son and his son's mother and sent them on their way. And little Isaac, what did he understand of that day? He was probably five or six years old at the time. Little Isaac was losing a brother. In later years, did he come to understand that it was somehow his fault that Ishmael had to go? Did he call out as his brother disappeared over the horizon, "Goodbye"? Did Ishmael turn and wave?

Could you have sent them away?

Could you have sent them away?

Let us pray:

Loving God, give us the grace to imagine the world you intend. In Jesus Christ. Amen.

If You Were Shocked Last Sunday That Abraham Gave Away His First-Born Son, Wait Till You Hear Who He Gives Away Today!

Now there was a famine in the land, so Abraham went down to Egypt to sojourn there, for the famine was severe in the land. When he was about to enter Egypt, he said to Sarah, his wife, "I know that you are a woman beautiful to behold. And when the Egyptians see you, they will say 'This is his wife.' Then they will kill me, but they will let you live. Say you are my sister, that it may go well with me because of you and that my life may be spared on your account."

So when Abraham entered Egypt, the Egyptians saw that the woman was very beautiful. And when the princes of Pharaoh saw her, they praised her to Pharaoh and the woman was taken into Pharaoh's house. And for her sake he dealt well with Abraham. And he had sheep and oxen and he-asses, manservants, maidservants, and she-asses and camels.

But the Lord afflicted Pharaoh and his house with great plagues because of Sarah, Abraham's wife. So Pharaoh called Abraham and said, "What is this you have done to me? Why did you not tell me that she was your wife? Why did you say, 'She is my sister,' so that I took her for my wife? Now then, here is your wife. Take her and be gone." And Pharaoh gave orders concerning him and they set him on his way with his wife and with all that he had. Genesis 12: 10-20

When the For-Sale sign went up in my front yard, my neighbors began to stop and ask me where we were moving. When I'd be out in the yard, cutting the grass or pulling the weeds, a neighbor would pull over to the side of the road, roll down the car window, and motion me over. "Where are you moving?" And I would say, "I'm retiring soon and we're moving to California." And the response was always exactly the same: "California?" As though it were on another planet somewhere. "California!"

So this week when I was out cutting the grass and my neighbor pulled up to the edge of the road and rolled down his window and motioned me over, I knew what was coming. He said, "Where are you moving?" I said, "I'm retiring soon and we're moving to California." And I saw the look of shock and disbelief come across his face. And he said to me, "You're still working?"

Do I look that bad? Why didn't somebody say something? Well, with the little strength I have left this morning, I want to tell you a little more of the story of Abraham. Last week we heard the sad story of his expulsion of his first son Ishmael. Today's story may be even more shocking.

Abraham was God's chosen instrument to bless the whole world. To Abraham, God gave a promise, that his children would be a blessing to all the world. And when Abraham arrived in the land that God had promised him, lo and behold, a famine. And then we have this strange story in which Abraham gives his wife to Pharaoh. What is the moral of this story? Is the moral of this story that if you give your wife away, you'll be blessed with riches and prosperity? If that's the point, it's not a very good Mother's Day text.

There was a famine in the land. In those days, without much transportation, it was easier to take the family to the food than it was to bring the food to the family. So Abraham and his extended family make their way to Egypt, where there is food. On the way, there is this conversation. It's not a conversation really; it's a monologue on Abraham's part. He says to his wife, "You are a woman, beautiful to behold." Well that's nice, isn't it? Ladies, just a word of warning. Now, maybe your husband says that to you all the time, but I know if my wife said to me, "You are a husband handsome to behold," I would be just a little suspicious about what was coming next.

"You are a woman beautiful to behold," he told her. "But when we get to Egypt and they see how beautiful you are, they'll kill me! So when we get there, say that you're my sister." Now the narrator is very careful here. He gives us no evidence at all that Abraham will be killed. This is in Abraham's head. It's not in the story. And in fact as we'll see in a moment, when Abraham actually gets there, and even when they find out that Sarah is his wife, not his sister, they don't kill him. They continue to heap gifts upon him.

So what's going on here? "They will kill me," he says. "Say you're my sister." Well, maybe he was afraid, but could there be another motive there? She's very beautiful, and as a commodity, that makes her valuable. Anybody ever watched *Let's Make a Deal?* When they got to Egypt, he said, "Meet my sister."

But could there have been any other motive? I'm not going to insist on this. I'll leave it to your judgment; but the narrator is careful to tell us that Abraham receives a promise that he will be the father of a great people. But he also tells us that Sarah has given Abraham no child. Could that have had something to do with how willing Abraham seems to be to let her go? So you be the judge of Abraham's conduct.

Well, Pharaoh is indeed smitten by this beautiful woman, adopts her into his house as his wife. And everything goes all right for a while. He heaps gifts upon Abraham, his new wife's *brother*. And everything goes fine until the plagues begin.

In the ancient world, people believed that if there was a drought or a flood, if there were frogs or locusts, it must be a plague sent by God. We in our modern world have a different worldview. Jesus in fact taught us that the rain falls on the just and the unjust, that the sun shines on the good and on those who are not so good. So we don't interpret every little change of weather as God's immediate hand, but they did in those days. "Something's wrong here, we're getting plagues, what's the problem?"

How do you think Pharaoh learned that his new wife was actually Abraham's wife? Abraham surely didn't tell him. Do you think it's possible that for the first time, we hear, muted, very quiet, Sarah's voice? Do you think she could perhaps have let it slip? Maybe they were having a lovely dinner there, steak and baked potatoes, and she said, "Oh, this is my husband's – oops -- I mean my brother's favorite meal." Do you think we're hearing from Sarah here?

Does the Pharaoh kill Abraham? No. In fact, the Pharaoh says, "What have you done to me? This is wrong! We here in Egypt, we know this is wrong. We understand this is wrong." The Pharaoh of Egypt has a higher moral code, it seems, than Abraham. The Pharaoh knows this is wrong. And so, he packs them up. "Take your wife, go back home. And take everything you have, everything I've given you, take it all, and go!"

So Abraham starts home with a stupid grin on his face. The scam has worked more or less. Yes, he still has Sarah on his hands. But look at all the loot he has gained! And besides, since he still has Sarah, he can run the scam again on someone else! (And he does! Read Genesis chapter 12.)

What is the moral of this story? I'm going to give you three choices. Very briefly, Abraham is chosen by God. But maybe what this story means is that just because you're chosen by God doesn't give you a pass to do any old thing you want to do. Being chosen doesn't mean that the rules don't apply to you. Some of the greatest crimes ever committed in the history of the world were committed by people who believed that because they were on the good side, because they were on God's side, they could do anything they pleased. The rules still apply, even to Abraham. Maybe that's it.

Or, maybe the story simply demonstrates that God uses imperfect people. In other words, God can use people like us. Maybe that's the point.

Or maybe it's this: Sarah is part of God's plan. God intervenes to return Sarah to the family because the promise is not just to Abraham; it's to Abraham *and* Sarah! The promise is not just to fathers and sons and brothers, the promise is also to mothers and daughters and sisters. Sarah is not just a piece of property to be passed around. She is a woman of God's own choosing, just as Abraham is a man of God's own choosing. She is a partner in the covenant promise.

It has taken God's people a long time to get this idea about the role and place of women. Indeed, 20 centuries after Sarah, a son was born to a mother named Mary, and mothers and daughters then were not much better off than they were in Sarah's day. Jesus challenged the attitudes and prejudices that he encountered. He engaged women as equal partners in the family of God. And wherever the Gospel has been preached, the truth of Jesus' message has lifted mothers and daughters and sisters to a new level of dignity and honor.

Well, there is a postscript to the story. Abraham is sent on his way. Can you see him going home there, driving the new Ford pickup truck that Pharaoh has given him, pulling a couple of new Ski-Doos behind him. A flat-screen TV loaded in the truck bed. He's got it all, all the gifts. But there is one other very subtle detail. Did you notice it? He goes home with manservants and maidservants, he-asses, and she-asses. Maidservants, one of whom was a little Egyptian girl named Hagar.

Hagar would become -- if you were here last week you might remember-- Hagar would become the mother of Abraham's first child, Ishmael. Hagar, whose presence would bring Abraham heartbreaking conflict and sadness, she was part of the loot Abraham was so pleased to be taking home from Egypt.

Choices have consequences. And what Abraham eventually learns is that more often than we imagine, God gets the last word.

And God always gets the last laugh.

Let us pray: Loving God we thank you for what you have entrusted to us through the families that have blessed us. In Jesus Christ, Amen.

Beth Say A Duh

And they came to Bethsaida. And some people brought to Jesus a blind man and begged him to touch him. And he took the blind man by the hand and led him out of the village. When he had spit on his eyes and laid his hands upon him, he asked him, "Do you see anything?" And he looked up and said, "I see men, but they look like trees walking." Then again, he laid his hands upon his eyes and he looked intently and was restored, and saw everything clearly. Mark 8: 22-25

Let's do this together. On three. One, two, three. *Beth say a duh.* Bethsaida. You've got it. These Biblical names and places can be difficult to pronounce. Bethsaida. It's a little fishing village on the north shore of the Sea of Galilee, just down the road from the better-known town of Capernaum. Bethsaida was apparently the birthplace of Peter, Andrew, and Philip. The Roman governor Herod Philippi renamed the town about 30 A.D., just about the time that Jesus was there with his disciples. Herod renamed the town Julius, in honor of the wife of Caesar Augustus, the Roman emperor. So it must have been a lovely little town. It is one of those places that Mark's Gospel identifies as an important landmark on the road to Easter. Last week we looked at Mark's story about Nazareth. This week we are looking at Bethsaida.

Mark's Gospel is my favorite, not only because it is the briefest of the Gospels (you can read the whole thing in 30 or 35 minutes, and I invite you to do so) but also because it was probably the earliest written account of the life of Jesus. And Mark's Gospel is distinctive because of its colorful detail. The other Gospels are fine, I'm not being critical of the others, but Mark notices details that the other Gospels don't. He is almost brutally honest about what happens. His accounts of the disciples are not kind to the disciples. In Mark's Gospels, the disciples appear to be a kind of Keystone Kops, a bunch of clowns. They just don't get it, and over and over again we see Jesus' infinite patience with the bumblers that are following him. He is infinitely patient.

Now, the details of the story. Other Gospels have accounts of Jesus healing the blind. But so far as I know, only this account has this detail: Jesus took him by the hand, took him by the *hand*, led him down the road and out of the village. He took him by the hand, a tender detail. On Monday morning we awoke to tragic news from Chardon, Ohio, another school shooting. I watched the video from that morning, those parents arriving at the school not knowing the wellbeing of their own children. The students were released one at a time into the custody of their parents, but in every reunion that I saw, when their children came out the door, the parents touched them in some way, with a hug, a kiss, some sign of deep affection. Jesus took the man by the hand and led him out the road.

Then, and there's no easy way to say this, he spit; he spit in his eye. Now, a few weeks ago, we had another story in which Jesus used spittle, when he spat on the ground and made a little mud pie and put it on the blind man's eye. But this is a different story. In this story, Mark tells us that Jesus spit in the man's eye. That's what it says. Now, that sounds terrible to us, but it corresponds to an ancient intuition that there is something healing in saliva. And you all practice that when you hit your thumb with a hammer, you know? It seems to be an ancient reflex: we think saliva has some healing power. Your little granddaughter falls and scrapes her knee, and you bring her over and embrace her and say, "Let me kiss it. Let me kiss it." Same reflex. So, what Jesus does there is not that unusual. And he asks the man, "Can you see?" And the man responds, "Well, sort of. But not perfectly."

So, what kind of a story is that for Mark to tell? Jesus leads the man by the hand, makes the spittle, goes through the motions, touches his eyes, oops, it doesn't work. At least not completely. What kind of a story? The other Gospels don't tell this story. Mark is the only one. Matthew, Luke, John, don't tell this story. It's kind of embarrassing; Jesus didn't get it right the first time. Didn't get it all done. Mark tells it like it is. "Can you see?" "I can see people, but they look like trees walking." So Jesus touched his eyes again.

More than 40 years ago, I heard Dr. Richard Graves preach on this text, and for 40 years I have envied the title that he used for his sermon. I had to settle for *Beth Say A Duh*, but Dr. Graves titled this passage, *The Second Touch. The Second Touch.* And his theme was that many of us, at one time or another, have had the first touch. You're here this morning because you've had the first touch. You believe in God. You may have questions about your faith, you don't see it all clearly necessarily, but you're here. If you hadn't had the first touch, you would probably be out golfing this morning. (Oh, maybe that is not fair to golfers.) But I mean you are here because you have some interest in the spiritual life; you may have doubts once in a while or struggles, but you are here. You've had the first touch. Dr. Graves said that we ought to recognize this reality. But we can also have a second touch! Many of you here have known that second touch: an experience, or a moment, or a crisis in which, maybe gradually or maybe suddenly, you could see things clearly. The things of faith meant more to you, were more important. You understood it, you felt it more deeply. That's the reality of the second touch.

First touch is important. Don't belittle or despise the first touch! Sometimes this happens. I've known a few people who, once they have received the second touch, then disparage everything about the first touch. They say, "Now I get it: I used to be a member down at the First Presbyterian Church, but I just went through the motions down there. But now that I've joined Second Presbyterian Church, now I really get it, now I've found a truly spiritual church home!". Don't, don't do that. Don't disparage the first touch. It's important. But recognize that there is sometimes a second touch.

We're almost finished. When I was the pastor of the Leesburg Presbyterian Church in the little town of Leesburg, Pennsylvania, the church had a parsonage about half a mile down the road from the church. Between the parsonage and the church, there were probably nine or ten houses. The first house next to the parsonage was occupied by a Baptist family, my immediate neighbors; they were lovely people. We shared a driveway; never had any problems. Good people. The last house before you got to the church was a Methodist family.

Good people, nice people. I'll tell you more about them in a minute. But everybody in between the first house and the last house were all members of that Presbyterian congregation! And most Sunday mornings they would all be in church! Starting from the parsonage, the next house after the Baptist family belonged to Ellsworth and Gladys Martin, a gentle older couple, lovely people. Next after the Martins was Mrs. Kaufman, and she was really old. She was probably in her 70's when I was there. And she was something of a shut-in. She didn't get out very much, so she wasn't able to come to church all the time, but she kept up on everything. She knew all the church gossip and even initiated some of it. We discovered after we moved there that she was actually a distant relative of my wife. The next house was Bill and Sarah Mable Royal; they were very active. Sarah Mable was the Sunday School Superintendent, and Bill was the Chairman of the Trustees, so on those cold Pennsylvania winter nights when the furnace at the manse would go out, as it frequently did, Bill was the person that I'd call. He would come out at midnight if necessary, you know, and tinker with the furnace so the preacher would have heat. So the Royals, and then the next family was Barney and Vi Davis, and I'll come back to Barney and Vi in the minute. Then next were the Colberts, then the Philips, and then there was a barn and a cross-street, an intersection. After the intersection it was Bill and Pat Demine, then Bud and Martha Lizzy. Bud had a saw sharpening business; he sharpened saws for the Amish carpenters. And if you walked by in the evening when he was in his garage sharpening saws you would hear that grinding sound of steel against steel. It would set your spine tingling. But if it was a good saw and if Bud was just about finished with it, then it made a kind of sweet sound, steel on steel; it's hard to describe, but it sounded somehow melodic So Bud sharpened saws. Then the last house before the church belonged to the Tunstalls, the Methodist family. I got to know Dave Tunstall pretty well because he was right across the parking lot

(I know where I'm going with this, so just be patient.) One day I was in my office which was in the corner of the church closest to Dave Tunstall's house; I heard this ruckus outside and heard a voice calling, I thought saying, "Help, help!" I went outside to look and there was Dave up on a stepladder inside of his garage; his garage door was open so I could see him there, and he had his hand up in the air, and he was yelling, "Help, help me. Somebody comes and help." So I rushed over and said, "Dave, what's wrong?" He said, "I'm installing this new garage door and the darn thing opened and it's caught my finger up here and I can't get out. You are going to have to press the button to close the garage door to get my finger loose." So I said, "Are you sure you want me to do that?" "Yeah, yeah," he said, "that's the only way I am going to get loose." So I went and pressed the button and he cried out, but he was free. He was bleeding, so when his wife got home from wherever she was, she took him to the hospital and got him stitched up and he was okay. But if I hadn't come along, he might still be standing there on the ladder. Dave had a barrel, a steel barrel out at the back corner of his property where he put his grass clippings and his yard debris. Every once in a while, the thing got full and he'd set a match to it and burn it down a little bit, but it never burned down to the bottom; the barrel was about half full with dirt and ashes and various things. So one day as I was crossing the parking lot to get into my car to go home for lunch, I heard a noise in the barrel. I was curious. I approached the barrel, but I approached cautiously because I could hear, you know, that there was something rustling around in there. I didn't want to get too close because I didn't know what it was. Well, when I got three or four feet away Dave Tunstall's beagle appeared. And she put her front paws out over the rim of the barrel and just looked at me. Well, my first thought was, hey, that's too good of a dog to throw away. And then I realized, you know, that made no sense. So I went to Dave and said, "Dave, you know, your beagle is stuck in your garbage can out there." "Never mind" he said, "she has a new litter of puppies and that's where she goes to hide when she needs a rest. She'll get out when she is ready."

So that was the street that we lived on. There were a lot of Presbyterians on the other side of the street too, but I'll tell you about them another time. All those Presbyterians and the Baptists and the Methodists that bookended them, they went to church every Sunday morning. Everybody went to church. You could have robbed my neighborhood blind on a Sunday morning because everybody was at church. Except for Barney Davis.

Barney didn't come to church. His wife was very active in the church and she was a lovely person. And Barney was a lovely fellow, a great guy, you know, and I enjoyed his company when I visited them. Once upon a time he had been in church, took the vows, joined the church, but he just didn't come. He just didn't come anymore. And I didn't hold that against him, you know; he was a good guy and a good neighbor. But then I got a call one day that Barney was in the hospital. So I went to see him and he explained to me that he had a blood clot. The doctors who were treating him to dissolve his clot. I had a prayer with him. The next day, I got a call from his wife; he had had a second blood clot and wasn't doing very well. And then the third day, he had another blood clot. So about the fourth day they put Barney into intensive care. But after two or three days, his wife called me to report that Barney was critical. "They don't think Barney is going to last through the night," she told me. "They said it would be a miracle if he lasts through the night." We prayed; when she went back to the hospital the next morning, Barney was still with us. He was alive. The doctor said to her, "Don't get your hopes up, he won't last the day." Well, she stayed all day and Barney was still alive. But as she prepared to go home, the doctor said, "I don't think he'll be here in the morning."

This went on for 21 days. She would go there in the morning, the doctor would say, "He made it through the night, but he'll never live through the day." And she would go home at night, and the doc would say, "He'll be dead by morning." And the next morning, he was still alive. Finally, the doctor said to her, "Look we've figured out that his leg is throwing off blood clots and that's why we can't get him better; his only hope is if we amputate his leg, but he may not survive the surgery because he's in such bad shape. But that's his only hope." So Vi said, "Well, if that's what you have to do, do it." So, they amputated his leg well above the knee, about halfway between his knee and his hip. And of course he was in intensive care then for many more days until he could stabilize.

And then Barney began to recover. I visited him in the hospital and on each occasion, I could see he was getting better. Now he could communicate, he was off some of the heavy medication. So on a particular occasion as I visited with him, we had a prayer, but as I turned to go Barney grabbed onto my arm with a surprisingly firm grip for the month that he had had; he grabbed my arm and said, "Reverend, if I ever get out of this, I'll see you in church." And I said, "Oh, Barney, don't worry about that, you know, we're just anxious to see you home again and get better." And he said, "No. You will see me in church."

Well, he got well enough to go home. He went home and then it was weeks for his leg to heal. When it was sufficiently healed, he got fitted at the VA Hospital, got fitted with a state-of-the-art artificial leg. It was quite a piece of equipment, you know, because it had to have a knee and a knee joint and all that. When his leg had healed to the point he could strap on that leg, he was able to get around the house a little bit and learn to use the leg, which took several months.

But eventually the morning came, the Sunday morning, when Barney Davis appeared walking up the sidewalk toward the front door of the church. It was still a challenge because the church there has four or five pretty steep steps. I went out to greet Barney and Vi, and said, "Let me help you up the steps." "No, no," Barney said, I'm ok." First, he put his good leg up on the first step; then he put his cane up on the same step. That gave him enough leverage to swing the artificial leg up onto the step where the knee joint would lock in place. Then he would repeat the process for the second step. Good leg up, cane up, swing the new leg, lock in place. Next step. It was amazing to see.

In all the rest of the years that I had the privilege of serving that congregation, I could probably count on one hand the number of Sundays that Barney missed. He was there every Sunday. Now I'm not suggesting for a minute that you have to come to church to be a Christian. I'm not saying that for a minute. But that was an important part of what faith meant for Barney. For Barney, it meant that on the Lord's Day he would be in the Lord's House sitting beside the wife the Lord had given him, worshipping with the friends and neighbors who loved him. That's what it meant for Barney. And I'm sure that if we could measure up all the years of his life before he got sick, and all the years of his life after he got better, Barney came to church more often on one leg than he had ever come on two. It was the second touch.

Let us pray.

Loving God, make us aware of and create in us an expectancy for yet another touch. In Jesus Christ. Amen.

What Were They Thinking?

When the teacher came up and heard them disputing with one another and seeing that Jesus answered them well, he asked Him, "Which commandment is first of all?" Jesus answered, "The first is 'Hear, O Israel, the Lord our God, the Lord is one. And you shall love the Lord your God with all your heart and with all your soul and with all your mind and with all your strength.' The second is this: 'You shall love your neighbor as yourself.' There is no other commandment greater than these." The teacher said to Him, "You are right, Teacher. You have truly said that God is one and there is no other but he. And to love him with all the heart and with all the understanding and with all the strength, and to love one's neighbor as oneself is much more than all the burnt offerings and sacrifices." When Jesus saw that he answered wisely, He said to him, "You are not far from the Kingdom of God." And the common people heard him gladly. Mark 12: 28-34, 37

When I saw the new uniforms the American Olympic Team will be wearing on Tuesday night at the opening ceremonies, I said to myself, "Wouldn't our deacons look good in those uniforms? They wouldn't have to wear the beret, but those snappy blue blazers and those smartly tailored slacks? We could buy a tailored uniform for each of our deacons. The uniforms only cost $1200 apiece!" I haven't discussed this yet with the Finance Committee, but I'm sure I could talk them into it. You never get a second chance to make a first impression!

What do you think of that? Unless you've been living on another planet, you're aware that there has been a controversy about the uniforms. It has to do not so much with the cost, but with the fact that they were manufactured in China. My own objection, I guess, to the uniform is that the Polo logo is on the left over the heart, and the American flag is over on the right side. And the flag is smaller than the Polo guy. So when our Olympians hear the national anthem, when they pledge allegiance to the flag and place their hands over their hearts, it might look like they are pledging allegiance to Ralph Lauren rather than to the American flag.

When we all heard that the American Olympic Committee had decided to buy uniforms made in China, some of us said to ourselves -- you say it, go ahead and say it -- "What were they thinking?" Indeed.

But of course there is a back-story. Now the back-story isn't going to change your mind about whether this was a good decision or not, but it's interesting. There is a back-story. *Ralph Lauren* is an American company, after all. And Ralph Lauren the man was born in the Bronx, New York City, USA, in 1939. He was born to Jewish immigrant parents who fled Belarus to come to the United States of America. His parents came here to escape the persecution sweeping across Europe at that time. They came to America, the city set on a hill, so that their children would have the freedom and opportunity that marks the promise of this country. Ralph's father Frank was not a wealthy man. He was an immigrant. They arrived on the shores of the United States with nothing. Frank became a house painter so that he could put food on the table for his family. But Ralph Lauren's family believed that education was the key to progress, so they saw that their three children were educated. Ralph finished high school, but before he went to college, he enlisted in the United States Army. Ralph Lauren is a veteran of the United States Army.

When he got home from the Army, he completed his college degree and went to work for Brooks Brothers, a great American company. And his job there was selling ties. And he was so good at it that he developed his own line of neckties: Ralph Lauren-designed neckties. And that's where he designed this little logo, the guy on the polo pony; that's where that started. And he was so successful that he started his own company. In 2009, *Ralph Lauren* revenues were over five billion dollars.

In 1964, Ralph married Ricky Ann, who was a nice Christian girl, a fact that Ralph hid from his Jewish mother for many years. Ralph and Ricky Ann are celebrating their 48th wedding anniversary this year. Together they raised three children. The oldest is in Hollywood, a filmmaker and director. Their second son recently married the granddaughter of former president George H. W. Bush. You might remember reading that in the paper not long ago. And their third child runs Dylan's Candy Bar in New York City. Who's been to Dylan's Candy Bar? Reportedly it's the largest candy store in the world. Daughter of Ralph Lauren. Aren't you glad you're here this morning?

Ralph Lauren and Company might have been, you know, the perfect choice for American Olympic Team uniforms. It's an American company, he's an American success story. Everything about it is just right. Except for that business about China. That's a little hard.

Ralph Lauren is successful worldwide and wealthy today, but it wasn't always that way. No, he started with nothing. His family started with nothing; they have lived the American Dream.

You can't see this because of my preaching robe, but I wore my Ralph Lauren shirt today. I only have one. I wore it not to show off, but in case any of you accidentally wore your Ralph Lauren clothes today, I didn't want you to feel conspicuous. I bought my Ralph Lauren shirt off the clearance rack down at the mall. It was about 80% off. And when I got home, I realized why it was on the clearance rack. I said to my wife, "Honey, they forgot to sew the pocket on this shirt! There's no place to carry your pens and your chewing gum. There's no pocket." And she patiently explained to me, as you probably already know, that high-end designer shirts never have pockets. Apparently if you can afford a Ralph Lauren shirt, then you can afford to hire someone to carry your pens in the pockets of his cheap shirt. All right.

If somebody asks you this afternoon what the sermon was about this morning, please don't say it was about Ralph Lauren. Folks just wouldn't understand. Say instead that the message was about the simple goodness of ordinary people. That's what I want you to think about today. That's what our scripture lesson is about. It's about the simple goodness of ordinary people. And if somebody asks you for a little more information about the sermon, say that our Lord Jesus awakened and celebrated the simple goodness of ordinary people. Jesus' ministry was not with the high and mighty. There were, here and there, a few well-to-do individuals who recognized the value of his ministry (Joseph of Arimathea and Lydia and some others). But by and large the ministry of Jesus was with shopkeepers and carpenters, with farmers and fisherman, with ordinary people, and often with the wretchedly poor.

Jesus kept the company of ordinary people. He loved them, he touched them, he healed them, he cared for them. And his caring awakened in them a simple goodness. "What is the law?" the scribes asked him. It's not so complicated. It's not easy, but it's not complicated. "To love the Lord your God with all your heart and with all your strength and all your understanding, and to love your neighbor as yourself." And ordinary people, Mark tells us, heard him gladly. They recognized that in Jesus, they had a friend. It was true then, and it's true today.

I told you a few weeks ago about the little town of Leesburg where I began my professional ministry. Now Leesburg, Pennsylvania, is nothing like Leesburg, Virginia, or Leesburg, Georgia. The Leesburg where I started out is just a straight little piece of highway with homes on one side of the street and mostly small businesses on the other. That's it. Probably never more than 100 people living in the town at one time. By the way, I take the time to tell you this because many of you grew up in "Leesburg". Everybody knows somebody who grew up in a place like Leesburg. The town is so small that the "Welcome to Leesburg" sign coming in from the south and the "Welcome to Leesburg" sign coming in from the north are on the same post.

And at one end of town is the Presbyterian Church and at the other end of the town is the Presbyterian parsonage where my wife and I lived. And in between on the east side of the road, are all these houses, ten or twelve houses, most of whom are Presbyterians and members of that church. I told you about that a few weeks ago.

But I didn't tell you about the other side of the street. There were two or three houses on the other side of the street. Stanley Cotton lived on the other side of the street. He was the largest landowner in the area. Not much of a churchman, but generous and supportive of the church. Stanley gave the land behind the church that became the new Leesburg Presbyterian Church Cemetery. Stanley was a good friend of all the community.

So Mr. Cotton lived there at the end of town, and then coming back -- well, there weren't many houses because the west side of town was the business district. And the business district consisted of the funeral parlor and the gas station. That was the business district. Now the funeral parlor was the Cunningham-Smith Funeral Home. Kenny Smith married into the Cunningham funeral home family, and Kenny ran the funeral home. And he was the best dresser in town. You know, Kenny believed that he would never get a second chance to make a first impression. And he was a sharp dresser. It's funny the things that you remember. He had funeral director's black shoes, shiny and nice. But Kenny's black shoes at that space right above your toes, you know, in front of the tongue of your shoes --white. Designer white. (I don't know what you call those shoes.) Almost everything I know about conducting a funeral I learned from Kenny Smith. I never had a course in seminary about how to do a funeral or a wedding. Some of you are saying, "Now, that explains a lot." Kenny took me under his wing. I was a young, green pastor, and he took me patiently under his wing and showed me how to do it, and how to interact with grieving people. And he was greatly beloved in that community.

And next door was the gas station, the Leesburg Independent Service Station. Now it was housed in a little old building which at one time had been a Quaker State gas station. Now who remembers Quaker State? If you don't, Quaker State stations, at least up north, were built like a little cottage. They would have a gabled roof, a distinctive-looking little building. Quaker State had long since abandoned the station, and it was now independently owned by the Curfman family, Ned and Agnes. They were members of the Presbyterian Church; both of them at different times were elders and deacons in the church. They were very active in the church. And they operated the Leesburg Independent Service Station, which was a Seven-Eleven before there was anything like a Seven-Eleven.

It was a place where you could buy bread or milk or eggs as well as your gas. You could buy anything you needed there from popsicles to shotgun shells. And if he didn't have it in stock, Agnes would have it for you tomorrow morning. Ned worked in the garage fixing people's cars. And on those snowy winter mornings in Pennsylvania, I'd hear Ned in his snowplow truck plowing out the neighbors' driveways and the parking lots at the funeral home and the church. But he always started with the parsonage driveway so that I wouldn't be late to the office. As far as I know, he never charged anyone a dime for the plowing. He just did it. That's the kind of people the Curfmans were.

They had four children -- I'll be done with this in a minute--they had four children. And from the time that each of those children in turn grew to the height where they could see into the cash drawer of the register, they were working at the station. And I remember seeing them there, stocking the shelves or sweeping up outside or working the cash register, waiting on customers. And there never were very many customers. I mean, it's just a small town. The success that you gained from a place like the Leesburg Independent Service Station was not the kind of success that you'd take to the bank. It was the kind of success that pays off in the love and affection of your neighbors and in the respect of the people who know you.

Those kids, each one in turn, took their turn working in that gas station, and then they went home at night and worked in Agnes' huge garden. They raised a garden to help make ends meet, keep the family fed. A hard-working family. And I want to close by telling you where those four kids are today.

Somehow, I don't know how, but somehow Ned and Agnes sent those four kids to college. Mark, the oldest, works for SkillPath Executive Training Services today. Mark travels across the country from one end to another teaching seminars to young people, teaching them how they can succeed in business. SkillPath Executive Training, that's what Mark is doing. Sue, the oldest of the two daughters, is a physical therapist in Virginia. She works with people after they've had a stroke or an accident or injury to help them regain their self-confidence and their abilities. And besides that, she teaches physical therapy at the local college. Bruce, the third of the children, is a civil engineer working for the Peoples' Natural Gas Company. Bruce is the guy they send out when somebody reports a gas leak or when there's been an accident somewhere and they're concerned about the underground pipeline. Bruce is the troubleshooter they send out to keep the community safe. Jill was the youngest of the children. She was out in Hollywood for a time where she worked with a movie studio in the prop department. At one point, she worked with Burt Reynolds, provided the props that Burt was using in his film. But that wasn't a lifetime career. She went on to school and Jill is an attorney now. She works in the prosecutor's office in Winchester, Virginia. That's what has become of the Curfman children. That's what the Leesburg Independent Service Station gave us: that family, those kids.

I don't know how the Olympic Committee is selected, or how that Committee decides on the uniforms for the Team. But when they do it again in a few years, I'd like to suggest that they contact the Curfmans for advice.

Jesus awakened and celebrated the simple goodness of ordinary people.
They heard him gladly. Common folks found in him a true friend. That was true then, and it's true today.

Let us pray:

Loving God, we thank you for the example of folks who have worked hard and been faithful to their responsibilities. We thank you for the fact that our Lord humbled himself to come among us, to live and to love and to heal us.

In Jesus Christ, Amen.

You Don't See That Every Day!

Soon afterward Jesus went to a city called Nain, and his disciples and a great crowd went with him. As he drew near to the gate of the city beyond, a man who had died was being carried out, the only son of his mother and she was a widow. And a large crowd from the city was with her.

When the Lord saw her, he had compassion on her and said, "Do not weep." And he came and touched the bier and the bearers stood still. He said, "Young man, I say to you, arise." And the dead man sat up and began to speak. And he gave him to his mother. Fear seized them all and they glorified God, saying, "A great prophet has risen among us and God has visited his people." And this report concerning him spread through the whole of Judea and all the surrounding country.

Now the disciples of John the Baptist told him about these things and John, calling to him two of his disciples, sent them to the Lord, saying, "Are you he is to come, or shall we look for another?" And when the men had come to him, they said, "John the Baptist has sent us saying, 'Are you he who is to come, or shall we look for another?'" In that hour, Jesus cured many of diseases and plagues and evil spirits and on many that were blind he bestowed sight. And he answered them, "Go and tell John what you have seen and heard. The blind receive their sight, the lame walk, the lepers are cleansed, the deaf hear, the dead are raised, and the poor have good news preached to them. And blessed is the one who does not stumble over me."
Luke 7:11-23

Did you see the moon last night? You can see it again tonight, a full moon, more or less, again tonight. It is as close to the earth as it gets last night and tonight. That, by the way, is called the moon's *perigee*. Did you know that word? I had to look it up when I heard it. It's the moon's perigee, and the perigee is the opposite of the apogee. The apogee is when the moon is as far from us as it gets in its orbit, but today the moon is in its perigee. It is 17,000 miles closer than it is in its apogee. That's a big a distance. So the moon looks a little larger to our gaze and is a little brighter. And even though that only happens once a year,

Aren't You Glad You're Here This Morning?

I don't imagine that any of you were out at midnight last night saying to one another, "You don't see *that* every day!" But you don't see that every day.

That's not how we use that phrase. When we use the phrase "You don't see that every day," it has a little edge to it. The moon in its orbit is a natural thing. It waxes and wanes, it comes and goes, and it's explainable through the laws of science. But the things to which we say, "You don't see that every day" are more or less *un*explainable. You might use the phrase if you saw a man dressed in a gorilla suit driving his car down Cypress Gardens Boulevard. You might say to your friend, "You don't see that every day." We reserve that phrase for things that are out of the ordinary.

A few years ago I went to a memorial service for a beloved uncle in Pennsylvania. I was living in Ohio at the time, and it was a cold wintry day. I was not presiding at the memorial service, fortunately, because I was late. It was snowing, and the roads were icy so I didn't get to the church in time for the memorial service. But I called ahead and said that I was delayed and that I'd try to meet the family at the cemetery. As I drove into town, just as I was passing the cemetery, the funeral procession approached and turned into the cemetery. So I turned around and followed the procession to the gravesite. It was snowing hard by then, the wind was blowing, and it was cold. As people got out of their cars and struggled through the snow to the grave, they were all bundled up, scarves and hats and all. I did the same. But when I got to the grave and finally took a moment to look up from the snow, I realized that I didn't recognize a single one of the assembled mourners. I was at the wrong funeral! There I was, a stranger in their midst. And they were kind and hospitable, and thanked me for attending their loved one's funeral, especially in such bad weather. No one said, "You don't see that every day!" But, if on the way from the hearse to the grave the casket had opened and the deceased sat up and began to speak, or climbed out of the casket and walked around, *then* someone might have said, "You don't see *that* every day." Yeah.

And so that brings us to our story today. A most unusual story. And the response of the crowd to Jesus? I think there is an edge to it. When they said, "God has visited his people," I'm not sure that's really a statement of their faith at that point. I think they're saying, "You don't see that every day!" In Palestine in the first century, bodies were buried the very next day. They didn't have much choice. The bodies were always buried the next day. They were buried outside the city. You didn't bury people inside the city wall; the cemetery was always outside the city wall. Just as in our story today, the whole village would turn out for the parade out to the grave.

And the casket was not a casket really. It was a platform made out of poles and reeds woven to make a kind of a cot or pallet. The body would be wrapped in some kind of shroud and carried on the pallet on the shoulders of the bearers. If you've seen news footage of public funerals in the Middle East today, it's very much the same.

When the procession reached the spot where Jesus and his disciples were standing by the road, Jesus reached up and touched the wrapped body. And he said, "Wake up." The young man sat up and began to speak.

What do we make of this? Let's not insult the intelligence of this young man's family and friends; they thought he was dead. He was dead. This is a miracle. That's one way to look at this.

Many commentaries suggest an alternative: the young man was in a deep coma. Jesus awakened him. As recently as the late 19th century, comatose patients were often buried by mistake. There are many accounts from the English countryside in the 19th century of people who awakened in their caskets on the way to the cemetery. In fact, this was so common in England that a man named George Bateson invented a thing called the Life Revival Device, the Bateson Life Revival Device. It made him a wealthy man. And this is how it worked: you tied a string to the wrist of the corpse and ran the string up through the top of the casket and up through the ground to the surface, where it was attached to a little bell on a platform. Did you know this? And in those days, they called it Bateson's Belfry because of the bell on the top. In the event that a person had been mistakenly buried alive and awakened in the casket, he or she could pull the string and the bell would ring. So for several days after the funeral, members of the family would take turns sitting in the graveyard overnight to listen for the bell.

And this is where we get our English phrase *the graveyard shift*. Did you know that? This is all true. The graveyard shift. And if the bell would ring, then you would be *saved by the bell*. I always thought that phrase came from the boxing ring, but no. The origin of the phrase *saved by the bell* is Bateson's Belfry.

And what if the bell didn't ring? Then you've got *a dead ringer*.

This is all true. You can read about this in *The Great Train Robbery* by Michael Crichton. The book recounts what was, in those days, considered the "crime of the century," the great train robbery of 1855. In London they loaded £12,000 of gold bullion onto a train, transported it down the coast, then under armed guard, loaded it on a ship and sent it off to Paris. When it arrived in Paris the next day, the satchels that should have been full of gold were instead full of lead pellets. No gold; just lead. Crime of the century. And at the center of that crime was Bateson's Life Revival Device. The thieves had placed a casket on the train in the same baggage car as the gold. Inside the casket was one of the thieves, very much alive, with Bateson's bell attached. When it was safe and the guards were somewhere else, the "corpse" rang the bell, signaling his accomplices to enter the car and make the switch. This is all true, *The Great Train Robbery* by Michael Crichton. Aren't you glad you're here this morning?

Luke tells us this story. Don't get caught up in the science of it. The point of this story is that a young man on his way to the grave is called back to life. Whatever the details, he is called back to life. Luke tells this story to demonstrate the compassion of our Lord. Luke goes out of his way to tell us that the young man was the only son of his mother, and she was a widow. She had no one to care for her. She would be alone in the world, no one to provide for her. Jesus had compassion upon her and exercised his power. And I love the tenderness of this verse: Jesus called the young man back to life and "He gave him to his mother." He gave him to his mother.

Someone in the crowd that day might have said, "You don't see that every day." But instead they said, "God has visited his people." That was true then; it's true today.

God has indeed visited God's people. When a plane crashes and people lose their lives, someone inevitably asks about the will of God. But when a thousand planes land safely, it doesn't occur to most of us to ask if that's the will of God. When the diagnosis is cancer we begin to wrestle with the question of what God is doing, but when we're in relatively good health or when the healing process begins or when the healing process is underway, we don't think as much about the goodness of God. The goodness of God is hidden not in the shadows, but in the sunlight of life. Oh, I believe that you can find God in the shadows, in the hard places, but I also believe you can find the presence of God in the sunlight, in the joy, and in the blessings we all receive every day.

It's a hard idea to get our heads around. That's why Luke concludes his story with the conversation between the disciples of John the Baptist and Jesus. They see this miracle -- if you will -- or sign; they see it but they're still not convinced. They come to Jesus and ask him a question. And I love the way they ask the question. They don't say, "Excuse me, Sir, are you the one who is to come, or should we wait for another?" They say, "*John* has a question for you. This is John's question for you. He told us to ask, 'Are you the one?'" It's like when you go to your therapist and say, "Now, I have this friend who has a problem." Or go to your doctor and say, "I have a friend who has a ringing in her ears, but she's afraid to ask her doctor about it." No.

Jesus addresses the two men directly, and this is what he says: "The blind receive their sight, the deaf hear, the lame are made whole, the lepers are cleansed, the dead come to life, the good news is preached to the poor. Do you see it? Can't you see it? What are you looking for if not that?"

"Blessed is the one who does not stumble over me," he says. What do you stumble over? You stumble over stuff that's right in front of you. Stuff that you don't see. Jesus said, "Blessed is the one who doesn't stumble over me, because the truth that you're looking for is standing right in front of you." Don't stumble over it. God has visited God's people.

God has visited us. Nothing will separate us from the love of Christ. In all things God works for good. If we could only pry open the eyes of our hearts, we could see it day by day and blessing by blessing. God is at work along the dusty roads of life, calling us to life and giving us to one another for love's sake.

And that is something you *do* see every day.

Let us pray.

Loving God, open our eyes to that which is always before us: your life-giving presence.

In Jesus Christ, Amen.

The Standard Model, The Higgs Boson (Particle), And The Hadron Collider

In the beginning, God created the heavens and the earth. The earth was without form and void, and darkness was upon the face of the deep. The spirit of God was hovering over the face of the waters. And God said, "Let there be light," and there was light. And God saw that the light was good. And God separated the light from the darkness. God called the light "Day" and the darkness he called "Night." And there was evening, and there was morning, one day. Genesis 1: 1-5

We learned this week of the death of our friend Jim Knapp. Jim and his wife Elizabeth were long-time members of this church. Those of you who had the privilege of working with Jim and Elizabeth know how important they have been and what wonderful gifts they have given to this community of faith. So our sympathy is extended to Jim's family.

Jim had a distinguished career in applied science. Many of you know that he was a key member of the team that created the Hubble Telescope. That was just one of many significant accomplishments of Jim's fine career. And almost everything I know about particle physics I learned from Jim Knapp. And so I've chosen our subject this morning as my way of saying "Thank you" again to Jim and to remember and honor him.

All right, are you ready? We should start with the Standard Model. The Standard Model is a mathematical formula intended to explain and predict the behavior of atoms. An atom, of course, is the primary building block of all creation. And what is called the Standard Model is an equation, a formula, a recipe, you could say, for how to create a universe. And physicists have been working on the Standard Model for generations now, and it's a long-complicated thing. If we printed it, it would take two or three pages to print it all. It's very complicated, but it has a problem.

There's a problem with the Standard Model. And the best way to explain the problem is to imagine that you're going to bake a chocolate cake. You get your favorite recipe, and you get all the ingredients from the recipe. And you measure them out very carefully and quite precisely. And you mix it in exactly the order in which it's supposed to be mixed. And then you put it in the oven at exactly the right temperature and you bake it for just the precise amount of time that the recipe calls for. And you open the oven door, and out comes a chocolate cake.

But you're a scientist, and you know that one experiment does not confirm truth. And so you decide that you're going to make this chocolate cake 100 times. So each time you read the recipe, measure out the ingredients, and put it in the oven. When you open the oven door, there is your chocolate cake. But on the 73rd try, when you open the oven door, you find a lemon cream cake! So, you continue the experiment and you get more chocolate cakes and more chocolate cakes and more chocolate cakes, but on about the 97th try, you open the oven door, and there's an apple pie.

So you finish your 100th test. You've got 98 chocolate cakes, but you've also got one lemon cream cake and one apple pie. So being a person of science you say to yourself, "There's something about the recipe that I don't quite understand." And that's the problem with the Standard Model. Most of the time, it accurately predicts the behavior of chemical and physical reactions. Most of the time, it works out and produces chocolate cakes. But every once in a while: apple pie.

And so about thirty years ago, a Scottish physicist thought about this problem. And he said (Peter Higgs was his name), and he said to himself, "We're missing something. There's something about the Standard Model, there's something about our understanding of the behavior of the atom that we haven't identified yet." He theorized that there had to be a missing something not yet named or known, but essential to the behavior of the atom.

And so his fellow physicists read his work and thought he had a point there. They began to call this mysterious missing something the "Higgs Particle." They named it after Peter Higgs. And it was kind of a joke at first. But then, the more they talked about it and the more they thought about it, it became an accepted way of talking about this mysterious missing part of the recipe. The Higgs Particle.

(See, we're already two thirds of the way to the finish line this morning. We have talked about the Standard Model and the Higgs Particle. And now I need to tell you about the Hadron Collider.)

The Hadron Collider started to work in the summer of 2008, and at that time I told you a bit about the Hadron Collider. So if what I'm going to tell you next sounds familiar, you have an excellent memory. The Hadron Collider is basically a tunnel deep underground on the border between France and Switzerland. It's like a subway tunnel. It's circular, 17 miles around. And this is how it works:

> The physicists go to the starting gate where they have a little trolley-car. It's not really a trolley-car, but it's like one. It's a little vehicle. And they load up the trolley-car with a family of protons. A proton is a part of the atom. So they put all these protons in the trolley-car and start it off down the track. And as it goes down the track, it passes through a series of giant powerful magnets that are embedded in the tunnel wall. And so it goes down the tunnel and goes through the circular magnets, and every time it goes through a magnet, those protons sit up straight. It gets their attention. And as they go through successive magnets, the protons begin to line up behind one another, like beads on a string. And they get organized in the trolley-car. And then they go faster, faster, and faster. Not a hundred miles an hour, not a thousand miles an hour, but really fast. Almost as fast as the speed of light, traveling around through these magnets.

But that's only half of the experiment. The other half of the experiment is that there's a second trolley-car. And the physicists load up that second trolley-car with another family of protons. And they start it off down the track (This is the fun part!) in the opposite direction. And the second trolley-car goes through magnets like the first trolley-car. And the protons begin to sit up straight, and they begin to line up and it goes faster and faster in the opposite direction. Faster and faster and faster.

Until they smash together! They crash, and all of those protons lined up begin to crash into one another head-on. And there's an explosion. (This is so much fun.) Then the physicists begin to sort through the wreckage, the debris that results from this tremendous crash. What they're looking for in the wreckage, in the debris, is *evidence* of whatever it is they're looking for. And for the last four years, they've been looking for the Higgs Particle.

That's been the first project of the Hadron Collider. And on Wednesday of this past week -- you probably read about this or heard it in the news -- on Wednesday they called a press conference. All these physicists gathered there together in a room in Europe. And they announced their results of four years of crashing trolleys. And when they announced the results, people in the room stood in a spontaneous ovation. Applause. Tears falling from their cheeks. They'd found it! They'd found solid evidence of the Higgs Particle. Amazing! They found it. And so the 4th of July 2012, was an historic day in the history of .... religion!

You thought I was going to say, "Science." Yes, it's science too. But it was an historic day in the history of religious faith because we have cracked open the door just a little wider for the human mind to understand what God has done. God governs the universe. You thought religion and science were in competition, or even in conflict? Where did you get an idea like that?

Science was born in the church. Did you know that? Don't take my word for that. When you go home today, Google the names of the two monks working in the Sorbonne 700 years ago, Buridan and Oresme. You can check with me at the door for the spelling. Buridan and Oresme are widely credited as the fathers of modern science. Two monks working in the Sorbonne 700 years ago. John Calvin, the spiritual father of our branch of Christendom, wrote that "God has manifested himself in the formation of every part of the world, and daily presents himself to public view in such manner that our eyes can hardly open without beholding him."(From Calvin's *Institutes of the Christian Religion,* Volume One.) Science and faith are looking at the same reality, the creation that God has given us to enjoy as our earthly home.

So why the conflict? Well, just very briefly, for most of the last 400 years, science has worked under the philosophy called *Determinism*. Now Determinism in this context doesn't mean that you try really hard to do something. Determinism means, as it's applied in science, that the outcome of every event is *determined* by the laws of science. The weather or illness or whatever it is, it's all determined by the laws of nature and science. And we have picked this up in our daily conversation. We say, "What goes up *must* come down." We say, "You can't be in two places at once." Sure, common sense. The laws of science. We say, "It's easier to go around a solid object than it is to go through it," though some of us don't always learn that.

So, when we as modern people open our Bibles and read that Jesus walked on water, we say, as modern people, "No, it's impossible. There's something wrong there." It violates the laws of science as we know it. When we read that Jesus after the resurrection visits the disciples in the upper room, came through the door without opening the door, we say, "It's impossible!" When we say that Jesus healed people who had been ill, who had disabilities from the time of their births, when we hear that Jesus healed them with a touch or even with a word, we say, "Ah, it can't be! Violates the laws of science." When we hear that the dead are raised, we say "No, can't be." As modern people, we think these are impossibilities. But the more we learn about the atom, about how the fundamental building block of the universe seems to behave, the more we cast doubt upon that philosophy of Determinism. The atom doesn't seem to know that what goes up must come down. The atom doesn't seem to know that you can't be in two places at once. The atom doesn't seem to know that it's easier to go around an object than it is to go right through it.

My grandfather had a garage out behind his house, and the garage door was not one of those doors like we have, the modern door that goes up on a track and recedes overhead. His garage door was hung on a track with a couple of rollers holding it. And the door slid sideways. Who had a door like that? Anybody? Are you old enough that you had a door like that? It slid to the side.

So one day, my grandfather went in the side door of the garage and got in his car and started it. He was going to take my grandmother to the store or something. And my grandfather never really used his rearview mirror. We were always careful because when he put the car in reverse, he never really looked back. So on this day, he got in the car, started the car, and began to back out of the garage without opening the garage door.

So the garage door, hanging on those rollers began to go up as his car backed out. The door banged against his back bumper. And then when he backed out a little further, the bottom of the door dragged along the back of his car, you know. And then as he backed out further, the bottom of the door dragged up onto the roof of the car and he kept backing out. And when he got far enough, the garage door began to come down against the windshield, across the windshield wipers, you know? And then it banged down on the hood of his car, and eventually when he'd backed out far enough, the garage door was released and swung back into place where it had been before he started. He got out of the car, going up to the house to get my grandmother, but she was on the porch. She had seen this all. And she said, "Charlie, you can't take the car out of the garage before you open the garage door." And he said, "I just did."
And that exchange was fairly typical of their relationship for all of their years together.

That's how atoms behave. They don't seem to know. The more we learn about the atom, the more we learn what we don't know. At the very foundation of reality is unpredictability, not determined outcome.

An atom is pretty small. If you could expand an atom, a hydrogen atom for example, to the point where the nucleus, the core of the atom is the size of a tennis ball, then the shell of that atom, the outer rim of that atom, would be four miles away. It would be four miles between the core, the nucleus, the center, and the outer shell. And in between, nothing. Nothing!

You see, that's the building block of reality. The wonder is not that Jesus could walk on water, the wonder is that you and I can walk on solid ground. Because there's nothing there! Four miles of empty space between the nucleus and the outer shell. It's a mystery. But scientists believe that the Higgs Particle, this missing something, has something to do with how that empty space is solid. Or at least solid enough for the universe to exist, how it has what's called *mass*, and how that empty space exists. And so the Higgs Particle has popularly been called the "God Particle." Not because there's anything divine about it, but because it answers a lot of questions. The Higgs Particle may make everything else possible. Without Higgs, the world, the universe, might collapse into nothingness. And so, the more we know, the more we realize how much we don't know.

Wednesday, July 4th, 2012 was a great day in the history of faith. For a moment, we have pushed open the door and glimpsed the immeasurably glorious wonder of God's creation. When it comes to understanding what God has given us here in this creation, we are a lot like children after a summer thunderstorm, splashing in the puddles while the great ocean of knowledge goes unexplored.

Do you know Tennyson's poem, "Flower in the Crannied Wall?" Alfred Lord Tennyson wrote these verses. Now first of all, you know what a crannied wall is, right? A little bit of old-time language. A stone wall isn't smooth, it has nooks and niches and crevices like your English muffin. Crannies. So:

Flower in the crannied wall,
I pluck you out of the crannies,
I hold you here, root and all, in my hand,
Little flower—but if I could understand
What you are, root and all, and all in all,
I should know what God and man is.

Let us pray:

Loving God, give us humility appropriate to the wonder of your creation. In Christ Jesus, Amen.

Elizabeth Blackwell And Elizabeth Wiley

So Jesus said to the woman, "Your faith has saved you. Go in peace." Soon afterward, he went on through the cities and villages preaching and bringing the good news of the Kingdom of God. And the twelve were with him, and also some women. Luke 7:50-8:1

I know this is a busy Sunday morning. Some of you are perhaps concerned about the length of our service today, and I'm aware of that concern. I just want to reassure you that I have no intention whatsoever of shortening my sermon.

Elizabeth Blackwell was born on the third of February in the year 1821 in the village of Counterslip, England. Her parents were Quakers. They had what, by the standards of the time, were fairly radical ideas. Her parents, for example, believed that girls should receive an education. Her father moved the family to the United States when Elizabeth was ten years old. And they settled in Cincinnati, Ohio, where he opened a business. But a few years later, both Elizabeth's father and mother died, leaving her to care for her brothers and sisters. Because she had been educated, Elizabeth was able to secure a teaching job in the town of Asheville, North Carolina. So she moved her brothers and sisters to Asheville and began teaching there. She followed the progressive religious ideals of her parents and included among her students the children of slaves.

Elizabeth had a dream. Growing in her heart and mind for many years had been the thought that perhaps God wanted her to become a doctor. And that dream continued to grow as she worked in Asheville. One evening, as she enjoyed the view from one of the mountains overlooking Asheville, suddenly, overwhelmingly, she was conscious of a Presence. She would later describe it as "a revealed experience of Truth, a direct vision of the great reality of spiritual existence." In *Elizabeth Blackwell: First Woman M.D.*, Nancy Kline records the effect of this moment on Elizabeth: "All doubt as to her future, all hesitation as to the wisdom of her dream, left her. She knew that however insignificant her small effort might turn out to be, that she was moving in the right direction in harmony with the purpose of the Divine Will for her life."

Then and there she resolved to become a doctor. (Kline's biography describes the many obstacles Elizabeth would face.) Elizabeth learned that it would take as much as $3,000 to get her through medical school, a huge sum of money at that time. But she had a wealthy friend who had promised her help whenever she needed it. And so, in humility she went to this friend one day and explained her dream and the cost of her dream. She asked if he could help. He was supportive of her idea. He encouraged her. Yes, he would help her achieve her dream, and he was prepared right then and there to give her a loan for $100.

So Elizabeth went on teaching for a number of years, saving what little money she could save until it was time to apply to medical school. Finally that day arrived. She sent off her first application and, in a few weeks, a letter came back. She had been rejected. She applied to a second school, and a third, and a fourth, and a fifth. Some of the letters returned to her were polite. Others were dismissive. "No, we don't accept women into our medical college." She applied to 16 medical schools and was rejected by 16 medical schools. At last, she applied to a little school in the town of Geneva, New York, the Geneva College of Medicine. When the Dean received her letter, he didn't know what to make of it. He called a meeting of the student body and read her application letter to the assembled students amidst their laughter and ridicule. They thought it was a joke. The Dean said, "I'll leave this decision in your hands as a student body." The students thought that some other neighboring medical school had concocted this thing as a way to ridicule their school. So someone raised a hand and moved that the application be accepted. And another seconded it. And before long, there was a unanimous vote to receive her. They thought it was a joke! How surprised they were a few weeks later when Elizabeth arrived to attend class.

For the first few months, Elizabeth was not permitted in some of the more controversial classes -- anatomy, for example, or the classes where they actually worked with cadavers. But she was patient and insistent that she be treated like any other student. And so, there she was, a student of medicine.

Aren't You Glad You're Here This Morning?

Now the community there viewed her with suspicion. She was not welcomed, even in the town, let alone in the classroom. But she persisted. She was patient. She worked hard. And three years later, Elizabeth Blackwell graduated from medical school first in her class! You saw that coming?

The graduation ceremonies in Geneva, New York took place in the local Presbyterian Church. I called that Presbyterian Church this week because it piqued my curiosity. The church secretary answered the phone, a lovely person. And I said, "Is this the Presbyterian Church of Geneva, New York?" And she said, "Yes." I said, "Do you know about Elizabeth Blackwell?" And she said, "Well, of course!" And I said, "Well, your congregation is aware of the historic nature of your congregation's role?" And she said, "Of course; do you want me to send you a brochure?" And I said, "Yeah, sure!" So she's going to send us a brochure, and I'll put it out on the narthex table next week.

I learned just this morning that our excellent organist Phillip has been in that Church! Phillip knows all about Geneva, New York, and Hobart College, which is the successor to the Geneva College of Medicine. Isn't that interesting?

So I said to the secretary, "Well you must be in a different location now than you were all those years ago?" And she said, "No, we're still here." I said, "Well, you must be in a different building." And she said, "No, we're still in the same sanctuary where Elizabeth graduated." She said, "We sit on the same pews they sat on the day Elizabeth Blackwell graduated from medical school, the first woman in the history of America to graduate with a medical degree."

On the day of graduation, Elizabeth walked to the church alone except for the company of her brother. She had been isolated in that community for a long time. As she neared the Church, she grew increasingly anxious because there was not a soul on the street. She thought that perhaps the townspeople had decided to boycott the whole affair because of her presence in the graduating class. But as her brother opened the door into the narthex of the Presbyterian Church, Elizabeth was greeted by a spontaneous outburst of cheering and applause. Every seat in the sanctuary was filled, mostly with the women of that community. Women had come from miles away to share her moment of triumph, to rejoice with her, and to congratulate her on her achievement.

Elizabeth Blackwell went on to have a successful career in medicine. She studied in London and then in Paris, returned to New York City, where she opened a clinic, which has survived to this day. It has become the New York Infirmary for Women and Children. If you've ever been to a pediatrician, you are a beneficiary of the pioneering work of Elizabeth Blackwell.

Though she remained single all her life, she adopted a daughter. And her daughter became a doctor. Together they opened a school for nursing in New York. That school trained many of the nurses who went out to serve the wounded soldiers on the battlefields of the American Civil War. Her achievements touched thousands, even millions of people. Elizabeth Blackwell. And she undertook this great work of healing because she understood that God was calling her to it. And she remained faithful to that calling all of her life.

I thought you might enjoy remembering her story on this Mother's Day. But that's not quite the whole story. There's a little bit more. At the very same moment in history when Elizabeth Blackwell was being rejected in her applications to medical school, there was another young woman half a continent away who was having the same experience of rejection. At the same moment that Elizabeth Blackwell began her practice in New York City, there was another young woman out in the middle of the country who was opening her practice of medicine. History has almost forgotten her. Elizabeth Blackwell was in London and Paris and New York; the world noted and remembered her. She was in the bright lights of Broadway and in the pages of East Coast newspapers.

But Elizabeth Wiley was born in Kent, Indiana. She lived on a farm. She was expected to grow up and spend her life sewing and cooking and raising kids. She lived out on the frontier. But when Elizabeth Wiley was fourteen years old, her mother was stricken with typhoid. And she tended to her mother during her sickness. Elizabeth Wiley said to herself, "I can honor the memory of my mother by becoming a doctor."

And so quite independent of Elizabeth Blackwell on the East Coast, Elizabeth Wiley set off on this same course. She studied, educated herself in spite of the rejections. Finally, years later, she was granted a medical degree by the University of Michigan. Elizabeth Wiley served patients in the Midwest and then moved her practice all the way to San Francisco, all the way on the West Coast. And the world has almost forgotten her.

If you look in the encyclopedia today for Elizabeth Wiley Corbett (Corbett was her married name), you won't find anything. Jim Corbett is there – the boxer, you know? Remember Gentleman Jim Corbett? He's there, but not Elizabeth Wiley Corbett. I went to the library; I looked at every encyclopedia they have at the Winter Haven Public Library. She's not there. She's not there! If you Google (and I can't believe I say that as often as I do anymore) but if you Google America's first woman doctor, Elizabeth Blackwell's name comes up. There are pages and pages and articles and articles about America's first woman doctor, Elizabeth Blackwell. And it's well deserved. But Elizabeth Wiley's achievement was no less heroic and no less worthy of being remembered. The circumstances of her life did not grant her fame or fortune or notoriety. She lived in quiet dignity all of her life. And she is *not* forgotten. One careful historian remembered.

If you Google Elizabeth Wiley Corbett, one article appears. Just one. And as I read that article, I said to myself, "I recognize those words. I've read those words before." So I went to a book that's on my bookshelf, opened it, and found the exact same article. The biography that appears on the internet is taken verbatim from the book *Great Scots!* written by James Thomson of Winter Haven, Florida. Jim Thomson remembered! He wrote her story. He did the research. Jim lived in Chicago for many years; maybe he ventured over to Kent County, Indiana, to look for grandchildren or great-grandchildren, or to scour historical archives. Whatever means he may have employed, he found Elizabeth Wiley's story and saved it so the world would not forget her.

I have a copy of that book because Jim's wife Ruth gave it to me a couple of years after his death. You see, Jim and Ruth Thomson were members here, members of this congregation!

The golden thread of remembrance connects us to people and to places that we can hardly imagine. If you take hold of that golden thread right here in this very sanctuary, it will lead you on to Indiana, to San Francisco, to all those countless young men and women who are in the medical profession today because of the extraordinary heroism of two women, Elizabeth Blackwell and Elizabeth Wiley Corbett.

It's Mother's Day. It's a day for grateful remembering. And when we remember with gratitude, who knows where it will take us, or what we may discover?

Let us pray:

We thank you, O God, for the heritage we have, and for the way in which your love connects us not only to one another, but also to the loved ones who are at home in you, yet mysteriously present with us. Amen.

Two Churches, No Post Office, And A New Bridge

The next day Jesus decided to go to Galilee. And he found Philip and said to him, "Follow me." Now Philip was from Bethsaida, the city of Andrew and Peter. Philip found Nathaniel and said to him, "We have found him of whom Moses in the law and also the prophets wrote, Jesus of Nazareth, the son of Joseph." Nathaniel said to him, "Can anything good come out of Nazareth?" Philip answered him, "Come and see." John 1: 43-46

Merry Christmas. I know it's only May. When I read the scripture lesson it probably didn't occur to you to think of Christmas, but these little verses have an odd, but important connection to the Christmas story. Everybody in Jesus' day knew that the Messiah was to be of the House of David, the royal house, and David's royal house was centered in Bethlehem. So Messiah had to come from Bethlehem; everybody knew that. But Jesus was from Nazareth. His parents lived there before he was born. His parents raised him there. Jesus was from Nazareth. Everybody knew that. So, there's the problem.

Nathaniel may well be reflecting this expectation. Messiah is to come from Bethlehem. This has led some skeptics, when they read the Christmas story to say, "No way." All this business about Mary and Joseph going down to Bethlehem while she is nine months pregnant, you know, and the innkeeper, and no room in the inn, and the shepherds out in the field watching their flocks-- that's all a legend, the figment of someone's imagination to answer the question of how Jesus of Nazareth could be the Messiah.

But what we've learned in recent years is very interesting in answering the question. We know that up until about 100 years before Jesus was born, Nazareth didn't exist. It wasn't there. There was nothing there but a dusty hillside. And then about 100 years before the time of the birth of Jesus, the Hebrew community down in Jerusalem said, "You know, we need some of our people up there, up there in Galilee. We need some of our people up there." So they recruited volunteers and in about 100 B.C. a group of folks went from Jerusalem, from Judah, from Bethlehem, from all those towns down there in the south, up to the north and founded a new town, Nazareth. Now Nazareth because it was a new town needed people like carpenters. So it's no surprise that Joseph's family, carpenters, were up there. But when the time came for a birth, where would those folks go? They would go back home. Back to their roots. Back to where their family was. So now that we understand a little bit of the history of Nazareth, the Christmas story makes perfect sense.

The people of Nazareth were settlers. They were a colony up there in the north, deliberately resettled to increase the Jewish population there. Everybody in Nazareth was from somewhere else. Reminds me of Florida. With all due respect to those of you who were born and raised here in Florida, you must get tired of people asking, "Where are you from?" Where are you from? You're from here. But everybody in Nazareth was from somewhere else. And what happens in a community like that? And I worked on this sentence very hard, so listen up. Settlers in a colony very often find their identity as people more with the place that they came from than with the new place that they are in now. It takes generations to develop the loyalty to the new place. They are always from back home. And Nazareth was such a place. There were no great landmarks in Nazareth because there was no great history to mark. Nobody has roots in Nazareth. There were no statues in the town square of the town heroes because the town hadn't been around long enough to have heroes. It was just a dusty little hamlet on the back road to obscurity.

And this is what happens when settlers come to a new place. Think about the settlement of the American colonies. When the pilgrims came to Massachusetts Bay Colony and founded a community there, what did they name their town? Plymouth. (From England.) You know, they didn't think up a new name; they named it after the place they were familiar with back in England. When they settled the land which came to be Connecticut, they called their town New London. When they settled the territory that became the next state south, they said, "Oh this is a lovely harbor here; we'll call this place New York. When the area around my hometown in western Pennsylvania was settled, they named it New Castle (Newcastle). German settlers in eastern Pennsylvania named their towns Berlin and Hamburg and Mannheim.

Can anything good come out of Nazareth? When Nathaniel asks that question, he doesn't mean that Nazareth is a bad place. There is nothing wrong with it. It's just that there's almost nothing there. It's a new community; it's a settlement. Can anything good come from such a place? And then Philip says, "Come and see."

Come and see. And I think that is just about the most radical invitation that anybody ever received to the Christian faith. And I use the word radical on purpose. Philip told Nathaniel to come and see for himself. You have eyes and ears. You have a brain. You have a heart and a soul. Come and see. Test your own experience. That's a radical thought about how truth gets conveyed from one person to another. Not by the authority of the person speaking. Philip didn't say to Nathaniel, "Take my word for it." He didn't say to Nathaniel (as we sometimes say to our children), "Because I said so." No. He said, "You come and see. You come. You make up your own mind."

You are a person of value and worth. You are a person who has an opinion and you have a right to have your opinion. It's your opinion; you have a right to keep it; you have a right to change it when the facts that you discover lead you to change. You are an important person. You are a person created by God. I don't want to belabor this point too much, but when Philip says to Nathaniel, "Come and see," he is affirming Nathaniel's worth as a child of God. You come. You look at the evidence. You decide. You are important.

I make phone calls to other churches on occasion. And usually the questions that I ask those other churches are odd and obscure questions. And very often what happens is that the person who answers the phone says, "I can't answer that question; I'm only the church secretary." Or, "I don't know the answer; I'm only a volunteer." And that always bothers me a little bit. I want to say to our staff, "Don't ever say, 'I'm just the church secretary.'" No, you *are* the church secretary; you *are* the volunteer. Don't say, "I'm only." If you don't know the answer, then you don't know the answer, but don't belittle yourself. The Apostle Paul said, "Don't think of yourself more highly than you ought to think." But I think Paul would agree that you shouldn't think of yourself less highly than you ought to think. We all know people who go through life thinking, "I'm just a teacher. I'm only the principal. I'm only a corporal. I'm only a sergeant. I'm only a nurse.

I'm only the wife. (Or more appropriately) I'm only the husband." Don't do that. Don't think of yourself less highly than you ought to think.

I made a phone call this week in which I asked a difficult question. The young woman I was speaking with said to me, "I don't know the answer to that question, but I will find the answer for you." That's much better, you know; I like that; that's good. About 40 years ago, *Markings* was a best seller. Anybody remember that book? Dag Hammarskjold was one of the first Secretaries General of the United Nations. In his memoir, *Markings*, he offered an admonition I have not been able to forget. "Never," he wrote, "for the sake of peace and quiet, deny your own experience or existence." Never for the sake of peace and quiet deny your own experience or existence.

Can anything good come out of Nazareth? Yes, it can. Can anything good come out of ordinary places and ordinary people? Yes. It can. It's fascinating to me that, in spite of what we now know about Nazareth and its reputation as a no-account, one-stop-sign town, Jesus was known then and is remembered today as Jesus *of Nazareth*. Can anything good come out of Nazareth? Oh yes.

Alright, I've got one more story to tell you. And then we'll be done. Last Sunday, I told you about America's first woman doctor, Elizabeth Blackwell. If you were here, I hope you remember a bit of that. At the same moment of history that Elizabeth Blackwell was becoming America's first woman doctor out on the East Coast, in the Midwest, in the state of Indiana, Elizabeth Wiley was becoming America's other first woman doctor. They became doctors at almost the same moment. But Elizabeth Wiley's story has been largely forgotten because she was way out there on a farm in Indiana. She is remembered in large part because of the work of a member of this congregation, now in heaven, Jim Thomson.

I told you last week about Jim Thomson's book in which he rediscovered the story of Elizabeth Wiley. This week I called the historical society of Jefferson County, Indiana, to see if I could learn anything more about Elizabeth Wiley and her family. I knew that Elizabeth Wiley's father was a schoolteacher, a public schoolteacher, the only public schoolteacher for miles around. And I knew that he was a Presbyterian. The Wileys were a strong Presbyterian family who valued their faith and valued education. So I was talking with the chief archivist there at the historical society of Jefferson County, and I said, "Can you tell me anything more about Elizabeth Wiley?" And he said, "Who is Elizabeth?" We'd been talking about the Wiley family, but that was the first time I had used her name. And I said, "Well, you don't know the story of Elizabeth Wiley?" And he said, "No, no, I don't think we do." Now understand, this is the county where she grew up. So I said, "Well, I've got some information here about Elizabeth Wiley, and I'll be glad to pass it on to you." He said, "Yes, I would appreciate it if you would." Then he said, "I've been talking to you about Harvey Wiley." And I said, "Yes, I know, Harvey Wiley was Elizabeth's brother." (You see, last Sunday I didn't have time to tell you about Harvey Wiley.)

Harvey Wiley's story is not forgotten. If you Google *Harvey Wiley,* lots of stuff will come up. Upon his death, Harvey was given the honor of burial at Arlington National Cemetery as a national hero. He was an important member of the Theodore Roosevelt Administration. He is well known in educational circles. And Harvey Wiley's career and accomplishments touch every one of us every day. Already this morning you have benefited from his work in a direct and immediate way.

Like his sister, Elizabeth, he was born in a log cabin and raised on the farm in Kent, Indiana. He went to Hanover College, but his education was interrupted by the Civil War (he volunteered). After the war, he finished school, earning a degree in chemistry. Then he taught chemistry at Indiana University, where he was the first professor in the history of chemistry to have a laboratory in his class. Harvey invented the chem lab! He taught at Harvard University for a while. Then there was a new college in Indiana putting together a faculty, so Harvey Wiley became one of the charter professors of what came to be known as Purdue University.

Harvey earned such acclaim as a chemistry professor that he was recruited to be the Chief Chemist for the Department of Agriculture in Washington, D.C., where he worked for twenty years. His particular field of interest was food and medicine. Harvey's work focused on the adulteration of food and medicine by foreign chemicals or foreign substances. It was no surprise, then, that Harvey Wiley was appointed America's first Director of the newly created Food and Drug Administration. Harvey wrote the first law that protected people by regulating the quality of food and of drugs. Because of Harvey's work, when you buy a jar of honey, you can be confident that it is all honey and not about half glucose, as it was in Harvey's day. When you buy olive oil, you can be sure that it is all olive oil and not about half cottonseed oil as it was when Harvey first analyzed it. When you buy Coca-Cola, you can be confident that there is now no cocaine in Coca-Cola, as there was when Harvey Wiley studied it. And when the Cola-Cola Company substituted a strong jolt of caffeine in place of the cocaine, Harvey said, "You know, you ought to tell people about the caffeine." And so, accuracy in product labeling was born. And when you give your children children's cough syrup, you can be confident that it is not laced with morphine, as it was before Harvey got to work.

Harvey Wiley contributed to Americans' safety and health in ways that we can hardly imagine. All of that from his little farm in Kent. Well, he retired after a great career. In retirement he went to work for a little-known woman's magazine, just an obscure little publication. They hired him as their chief product tester. The magazine came to be known as *Good Housekeeping*. If you've ever heard of the Good Housekeeping Seal of Approval, that was Harvey's idea. He was the man who held the stamp for the Good Housekeeping Seal of Approval.

I thought you'd want to know about Harvey Wiley. Harvey and his sister Elizabeth changed the course of American history. When I talked to the historical society, I asked the receptionist there if she had ever been in the little town of Kent, where Elizabeth and Harvey were born. She said, "Well, I've been through it." I said, "I'm curious; can you describe this important landmark in American history? Can you describe it for me?" And she said, "Yes: two churches, no post office, and a new bridge." "A new bridge?" I said. "Yes," she said. "The old bridge fell into the river a few years ago, and they had to build a new one."

Can anything good come out of Nazareth? Oh yes, yes it can. Come and see.

Let us pray.

Loving God, we thank you for the faithfulness of those who have gone before us, and we ask that in our times and in our places, you will keep us serving one another. And You. In Jesus Christ. Amen.

Jesus And The Little Girl

Then came one of the rulers of the synagogue, Jairus by name, and seeing Jesus, he fell at his feet and besought him saying, "My little daughter is at the point of death. Come and lay your hands on her so that she may be made well and live." And Jesus went with him. But while they were still speaking, there came from the ruler's house some who said, "Your daughter is dead; why trouble the teacher any further?" But ignoring what they said, Jesus said to the ruler of the synagogue, "Do not fear, only believe." And he allowed no one to follow him except Peter and James and John, the brother of James. When they came to the house of the ruler of the synagogue, they saw a tumult and people weeping and wailing loudly. When he entered, he said to them, "Why do you make tumult and weep, the child is not dead but sleeping." And they laughed at him. But he put them all outside and took the child's father and mother and those who were with him and went into where the child was. Taking her by the hand, he said to her, "Talitha cumi," which means, "Little girl, I say to you, arise." And immediately the little girl got up and walked. She was 12 years of age. And they were immediately overcome with amazement. He strictly charged them that no one should know of this. And he told them to give her something to eat. Mark 5; 22-24, 35-43

It's good to be back with you after two weeks away. I'm very grateful to the Reverend John Alford for graciously filling in the weeks that I was away, and to Holly for helping him here during worship. On Christmas morning, my wife and I flew out to Oakland, California, where we spent some time with our daughter. We had a wonderful time. But we were actually in the air on Christmas Day over the western United States at the same time that the incident was happening on the flight to Detroit. Our flight was not affected in any way. However, on the return trip, just a few minutes after takeoff, I noticed some commotion just across the aisle from where I was seated. When I looked, I realized that the gentleman seated there was in some distress; there was a clear odorless liquid pouring out of the overhead compartment onto his lap. He immediately called the flight attendant and, when she saw what was happening, she called her fellow flight attendants. For the next 90 seconds or so, there was a good deal of activity in the aisle beside him. As it turns out, one of the passengers seated nearby had placed her water bottle in her carry-on luggage, put it overhead, but hadn't secured the cap. She was greatly embarrassed, but the rest of us were all greatly relieved. So it's good to be back with you.

When the writers of the New Testament thought about the life of Jesus, they had to remember backwards. That is, they included the stories of the birth and infancy of Jesus because of the man he became. The writers of the New Testament didn't know him first as a child, they knew him first as a carpenter, and the son of a carpenter. They didn't know him first as the Lord of all creation and the son of God; it only occurred to them much later that he might be God's son. They knew him as a teacher and a friend and a companion and a man. And because of the kind of man he was, they remembered backwards. They asked questions. They asked to talk to his mother and to others who were familiar with the circumstances of his birth and background.

He was someone in whose presence strange and often wonderful things happened. Even in the very worst of circumstances, to be in the presence of Jesus meant that something strange and wonderful might happen. They were on the sea one night in a terrible storm. They feared they were all going to perish. And even in that extreme situation he spoke a word and there was peace on the sea and in their hearts. They were at the funeral of their friend Lazarus; there was weeping and mourning. People had given up hope. But when Jesus arrived something happened, and Lazarus was alive again. In the presence of Jesus, the blind were made to see and the deaf were made to hear, the lame to walk. In his presence, tax collectors and prostitutes became if not saints, at least seekers after sainthood.

And so in this story today, the ruler of the synagogue, Jairus by name, a man of some power and position comes to seek Jesus' help because his daughter is at the point of death. I don't know whether Jairus comes because he is a brave man or because he is terrified of what might happen in the hours ahead. Is it courage or fear? Courage, I think, because it required some sacrifice on his part to come to Jesus. Powerful elements of the established authorities didn't think much of Jesus. They were suspicious of him, resented him. For Jairus to come and kneel before this Jesus meant that he, Jairus, would "never work in that town again." You know? I told the folks in the early service that it would be as if Rush Limbaugh came to Nancy Pelosi to ask a favor. Or have it the other way around if you want, Nancy going to Rush. You see: the distance between them was too great for Jairus to ask Jesus for a favor. His standing in the community would certainly suffer.

And moreover, this is his *daughter*; you can understand him coming for a *son*. Sons were a gift of God. Daughters were somewhere between good sheep and good goats. But this man loved his daughter! And he calls her "my little daughter". We learn later that she is 12 years old. She wasn't much younger than Mary, the mother of Jesus, when she gave birth. But as a father myself, I think I probably understand what is going on in his head. "My little daughter?" Our children are always our children. No matter how old they grow. When we see them, even in adulthood, we see them learning to throw a baseball or learning to ride a bicycle. We see them in their first baseball uniform or their prom dress. We see them always as our precious children.

My little daughter is ill! And Jesus went with him. Those who knew Jesus were not surprised. But on the way, they received bad news, the worst news; someone coming from the house of Jairus blurted it out in that awkward way that many of us share bad news and then have to apologize later for our insensitivity. "She is dead," they said. She is gone; don't trouble the Master any further.

And then Jesus said something that I don't fully understand. He said, "Do not fear, only believe." But he didn't tell us what not to fear and he didn't tell us what to believe. He just said, "Do not fear." Did he mean, "Do not fear because no bad things will ever happen to those you love?" Surely, he didn't mean that. Because it's not true and we know it. Did he mean, "Do not fear because it will all turn out for the best in the end, and she will go to a better place, and someday you will meet again in heaven?" Did he mean that? Perhaps. But he didn't say that. Did he mean, "Do not fear what the coming hour will bring? Do not fear that you will never hear her voice again, that she will never again say, 'Daddy's home,' that you will never see her dance in the sunlight on the patio?" Did he mean not to fear all of those things that Jairus must have been fearing?

And then Jesus said, "Believe." Believe what? Believe in God? Perhaps. Believe that all things will turn out for the best? He didn't say what to believe. And the best I can make of it is something like this. He meant, I think, "Trust me." Trust Him. In the hours of darkness and sadness, sometimes that's all we have. "Trust me," he says, because fear closes the door to God. It closes the door to life, to opportunities. If our lives are governed by what we fear, what we are afraid to do, what we are afraid to try, what we are afraid to experience, doors close. Hear them shutting. Slamming shut.

Fear closes doors to life. Some of you know that I have been no fan of flying. Until our recent flight, I hadn't been on an airplane for 19 years. But not flying means there are some places you can't go in a limited amount of time. Fear closes the door. The folks who sat behind us on the plane, when they saw my wife and I come in and sit down, said, "Oh we're so glad there are adults sitting in front of us. On the first leg of our flight, there was a family with four children and they screamed the whole time." I said, "Well, you're in luck then. I only scream on takeoff and landing." Fear closes the door, believing pushes it open. Believing, the practice of believing, pushes open the door, gives God an opportunity to show us something new, something different, something wonderful.

Jesus said to this father in this moment of extremity, don't be afraid, don't close the door, believe. Keep the possibility open. Well, you know how the story ends. Jesus goes to the house. There is a tumult of weeping and wailing, but Jesus will not have a public spectacle. His mission is not for the sake of popularity with the crowds. He pushes the crowds away. He enters the house with the father and mother, and Peter, James, and John, three of his closest disciples. And what he does there is as quiet as a whisper and as simple as a human touch. He takes her by the hand, calls her to stand, to arise, and to return to life.

Now one of the most important details in this story is that, while the New Testament is written in Greek, there are two little words in this story that are not Greek. They are Aramaic, the language that Jesus actually spoke, the language that would have been spoken in that household that day. "*Talitha cumi.*" Little girl, arise. What happened in the room that day was seared into the memory of Peter, James, and John. We believe that Mark, the Gospel writer Mark, wrote his Gospel after interviewing Peter. Peter was there in the room that day. Peter remembered those Aramaic words. So while all the rest of the story is told in Greek, those two words come to us down across the centuries, "*Talitha cumi*". They come to us because everyone in the room that day, and especially that father and mother, would remember those words forever.

What happened we cannot say for sure. Was she just in a coma that no one recognized but Jesus? He called her to life again out of a coma? If you are comfortable with that, that's fine; there's nothing in the text that suggests otherwise. He said, "She's not dead, she's sleeping." But if you choose to believe that it was a genuine miracle, then so much the better for that. What does it mean for us. Frederick Buechner closes his treatment of this story in this way: "Little girl, arise. Old boy, arise. Old boys and girls with high blood pressure and arthritis, young girls and boys with tattoos and body piercing, you who believe and you who sometimes believe and sometimes don't believe, you who would give almost anything to believe if only you could, arise."

In the presence of Jesus, strange and often wonderful things happened. And still happen.

One other detail. Jesus said, "Give her something to eat." What a wonderful way to close this story. She's hungry. Give her something to eat.

No one in the room that day could have imagined the nourishment that Jesus Himself would provide. As we come again to the Lord's Table, we receive the true Bread, the Bread that brings us life.

Let us pray.

Loving God, help us to push open the doors of believing so that we may think new thoughts and know new things and experience your grace in new ways. In Jesus Christ. Amen.

The Young Man Who Learned To Speak For Himself

As he walked by, he saw a man blind from birth. His disciples asked him, "Rabbi, who sinned, this man or his parents, that he was born blind?" Jesus answered, "It was not that this man sinned, or his parents, but that the works of God might be made manifest in him. We must work the works of him who sent me while it is day; night comes, when no one can work. As long as I am in the world, I am the light of the world." As he said this, he spat on the ground and made clay of the spittle, and anointed the man's eyes with the clay, saying to him, "Go, wash in the Pool of Siloam" (which means "sent"). So he went and washed and came back seeing. The neighbors and those who had seen him before as a beggar, said, "Is not this the man who used to sit and beg?" Some said, "It is he"; but others said, "No, but he is like him." He said, "I am the man." They said to him, "Then how were your eyes opened?" He answered, "The man called Jesus made clay and anointed my eyes and said to me, 'Go to Siloam and wash'; so I went and washed and received my sight." They said to him, "Where is he?" He said, "I do not know."

They brought to the Pharisees the man who had formerly been blind. Now it was a Sabbath day when Jesus made the clay and opened his eyes. The Pharisees again asked him how he had received his sight. He said to them, "He put clay on my eyes, and I washed, and I see." Some of the Pharisees said, "This man is not from God, for he does not keep the Sabbath." But others said, "How can a man who is a sinner do such signs?" There was a division among them. So they again said to the blind man, "What do you say about him, since he opened your eyes?" He said, "He is a prophet."

They did not believe that he had been born blind and had received his sight, until they called the parents of the man who received his sight and asked them, "Is this your son, who you say was born blind? How then does he now see?" His parents answered, "We know that this is our son, and that he was born blind; but how he now sees we do not know, nor do we know who opened his eyes. Ask him; he is of age; he will speak for himself." John 9:1-21

There is one question we can deal with right away and take it off the table. It is the question that the neighbors asked: why is this man blind. Did he sin, or did his parents sin? And Jesus answered, "Wrong on both counts." Are illnesses or misfortunes a direct punishment from God? No, that's not how God works. So if you've ever wondered if some illness or misfortune that has befallen you or your loved one is a punishment from God, now you don't ever have to ask that question again. Jesus answered that question and the answer is, "No." So if you get indigestion this evening from eating too much pizza during the game today, you have only yourself to blame. Are you clear on that? If you are, we'll move on.

Jesus understood this man's blindness not as a punishment but as an opportunity. That's why I've chosen this story for today. He was a *young* man; both of his parents are still living. They make a point of insisting that he is "of age", which would have been unnecessary if he was obviously older. This is the story of a young man.

And I want you to notice the *movement* of the story. As the story begins, the young man is more or less helpless. He is blind; he is a beggar; he is *dependant* upon others for everything. But by the time we get to the end of the story he has received the gift of *independence*. He can provide for himself now. He can think for himself now. He can even *speak* for himself now. This is what we all hope for our children! This is what we hope and intend for young people here this morning. We hope you will grow toward a confident and responsible independence. We rejoice to see you become an individual who can think for yourself, speak for yourself, and *be* yourself!

So Jesus makes a *poultice*, a little mud pudding, and applies it to his eyes. This sounds strange to us, but it was not uncommon in Jesus' day to apply a poultice to a wound or an injury. (Anyone here ever use Ben-Gay?) So Jesus daubs the mud on his eyes, then sends him over to the Pool of Siloam to wash it off. And when he returns, he can see!

But what happens next—and I hope you noticed, because its kind of subtle – what happens next is that the onlookers, the neighbors, do what adults so often do in regard to young people: they ignore him. They begin to talk about him as if he wasn't even there! He might as well be invisible. "Isn't that the boy who…. didn't he used to be…. isn't he the son of…?" they asked. "It looks like him…No, that's not him, couldn't be." And finally the young man speaks for himself. "I am the man," he said. "I am me, and I am here. I am a person. I am myself."

And isn't that what we hope our young men and young women will say with self-assurance about themselves? We intend that you, like the young man in our story, will find the confidence to speak for yourself. "I am here and I am me."

So then they said to him," Where is Jesus?" He answered, I don't know." It's a good answer because it's a true answer. It takes courage to say, "I don't know," when you don't know. Young people don't know everything. But that doesn't mean that they don't know anything. I don't know everything. And I bet there are even a few of you who don't know everything. But that doesn't mean that we don't know *something*. They asked him where Jesus was, and he didn't know, so he said, "I don't know." Fine.

Then they asked him the more important question, "What do you say about him? He opened your eyes; who do you think he is?" And now, for perhaps the first time in his life, someone has asked his opinion about something important, and he has an opportunity to express his own opinion! He gets to say what he *believes*; he gets a chance to speak from his own *experience*. "He is a prophet," he says of Jesus. And while that's not everything there is to say about Jesus, that much is true; He is a prophet. So this young man in his innocence, in his first ten minutes of seeing, is able to see a truth that the experts and authorities could not see. Or refused to see.

I don't think it's a stretch to say that God intends us to raise our kids and nurture young women and men in a manner that enables them to share the path of this young man. Not dependence, but independence is our hope for you. We want you to think and speak for yourself, even if your thought and opinions are sometimes different from ours. Remember the story of the general who was asked by a reporter what his troops thought about a certain situation. "If I want my troops to have an opinion about this, "the General replied, "I'll issue them one."

Well, if that's your philosophy of childrearing, all I can say is "good luck." The young men and women in this sanctuary today are well on their way to mature independence. And that's why we are so grateful for the selfless and dedicated service of parents, volunteers, and leaders who have supported them in this congregation's ministries.

I want to close this morning by telling you just a bit about Charles. Charles was born in the town of Loudonville, Ohio. Who's been to Loudonville? Raise your hand. Okay, several of you. It's a lovely little community about twenty miles down the road from the church I served in central Ohio. Charles was born on a farm on August 29, 1876, the fourth of five children. Charles never did very well in school because his eyesight was quite poor. He couldn't see the blackboard while he was at school; and when he tried to study at night after the farm chores were done, candlelight and oil lamps were very little help for a boy with poor vision. But he was clever and curious; he loved to take things apart, see how they worked, and put them back together. And he was determined to get an education in spite of the obstacles in his path. So he made it through high school and applied to college in the neighboring town of Wooster, Ohio. Some of you will recognize that the College of Wooster is a Presbyterian college with a long history of excellence. In spite of his rather poor high school record, Charles was accepted and began his studies. He worked hard; but after a few months the strain on his eyes forced him to return to the farm to recover. He rested. But as soon as his eyesight had improved, he returned to Wooster. He wanted that education. His eyestrain required a second leave of absence. He rested, then returned. Finally, at the age of twenty-eight, Charles graduated from college with a degree in mechanical engineering.

Charles went to work for a new company called National Cash Register. He worked there for a few years, but his real interest was automobiles. It was 1910 and the auto industry was an exciting new frontier. The big problem with an automobile in 1910 was that to start the darn thing, you had to go around the front of the car, insert a crank, and "crank" the engine into action. I don't think there's anyone here old enough to have done that. But you probably know that the worst feature of that system was that if the engine actually started, and if you didn't let go of the crank at precisely the right instant, the now rotating crank broke your arm! So Charles thought about that problem. National Cash Register had a new electronic cash register. He thought about the new machine and wondered how it worked. He disassembled one of those new machines and located the little electrical switch that opened the cash register drawer. And he wondered what if. What if? So he took that little switch from the register and wired to it a key slot (think of the key slot in your front door). Then he wired that apparatus to the engine block of a car. He took his invention to the headquarters of the Cadillac Motor Company to try it out. And it worked! If you came to church today in an automobile that you didn't have to crank, you are the beneficiary of Charles' first invention. Charles, born on a farm, whose eyesight was so bad he hardly made it through high school, and couldn't get through college until he was twenty-eight years old – he got you to church this morning!

But Charles wasn't finished. The roads weren't very good then, and riding in a car was a bone-jarring ordeal. So Charles invented what we know as shock absorbers. Anyone here have shock absorbers on your car? And now that cars had electronic ignitions, you had to have a dependable source of stored electricity. The existing batteries in those days were virtually worthless. So Charles opened a laboratory in Dayton, Ohio, to work on that problem. The facility became the Dayton Engineering Laboratory Company. The name was later shortened to DELCO, a name you will recognize if you've ever bought a car battery. Charles invented the modern battery.

But Charles wasn't finished yet. He took an interest in locomotives. At that time locomotives were mostly powered by steam produced by burning wood or coal. Charles thought there must be a better way to do it. So he went to work and designed a two-cycle diesel powered engine. Soon, that engine was standard equipment for every locomotive built in America. And with some modifications, that engine soon became standard for large trucks, tractors, bulldozers, and other heavy-duty equipment. Diesel engine? Charles invented that.

But Charles wasn't finished. He signed on as a consultant for DuPont Chemical. He developed an interest in heating and cooling. He began to study a family of gasses known as fluorocarbons. He mixed them one-way and another, try this, try that; eventually he settled on a formula for a particular fluorocarbon. He named his new gas formula Freon. I'll bet you've heard of it. Then he designed a pump to circulate and re-circulate the Freon, connected that to a fan, and installed it in his house. So his house became the first air-conditioned house in America. He invented air-conditioning; it's become fairly popular, especially here in Florida.

But Charles, the farm boy who could hardly see the blackboard, wasn't finished. He developed an interest in medicine. He was troubled that so many children born prematurely died within a few days of birth. So he went to work in his laboratory and designed a device we know as an incubator. Literally millions of children are alive today because Charles cared and created a solution.

But Charles – Do you want to say it? – wasn't finished. He was fascinated by magnetism. He thought it might have some application in the field of medical diagnostics. So Charles designed a machine for the purpose of using magnetism to examine patients. We call this *magnetic resonance imaging*. Yes, Charles invented the MRI.

He wasn't finished. How long do you want to go this morning? Or do you want to come back after lunch? I have several more pages here, because by the end of his illustrious career, Charles held 186 U.S. patents, most of which are for things that you and I use every day and could not do without!

With the wealth that his inventions amassed, which was vast, Charles established a foundation. The primary beneficiary of that foundation is the Memorial Sloan-Kettering Cancer Center. Charles Kettering changed the world!

As a boy growing up on a farm in rural Ohio in the 1880's and 1890's, Charles Kettering had few if any of the comforts or advantages we take for granted today. And he couldn't see very well. But he didn't consider that a handicap; instead, he turned it into an opportunity. So the next time you're tempted to think that one person can't make a difference, or that you can't make a difference, remember Charles.

Let us pray.

Aren't You Glad You're Here This Morning?

Loving God, we think you for the young persons who are here today, and for the boundless promise of their lives. Give us the grace to encourage them along their way. In Jesus Christ. Amen.

Forgiveness. What It Is And What It Isn't

Now one of the Pharisees asked him to eat with him. So Jesus went into the Pharisee's house and took his place at the table. Behold a woman of the city who was a sinner, when she learned that Jesus was at table in the Pharisee's house, brought an alabaster flask of ointment. And standing behind him at his feet weeping, she began to wet his feet with her tears and wipe them with the hair of her head and kissed his feet and anointed them with the ointment. Now when the Pharisee who had invited Jesus saw this, he said to himself, "If this man were a prophet, he would have known who and what sort of woman this is who is touching him, for she is a sinner." And Jesus answering him said, "Simon, I have something to say to you." And he answered, "What is it, teacher?" And Jesus said, "A certain creditor had two debtors; one owed him five hundred denarii, the other fifty. When they could not pay, he forgave them both. Now which of them will love him more?" Simon answered, "The one I suppose to whom he forgave more." Jesus said to him, "You have judged rightly." Then turning toward the women, he said to Simon, "Do you see this woman? I entered your house, but you gave me no water for my feet. She has wet my feet with her tears and wiped them with her hair. You gave me no kiss, but from the time I came in, she has not ceased to kiss my feet. You did not anoint my head with oil, but she has anointed my feet with ointment. I tell you her sins, which are many, are forgiven; therefore she loved much. But he who is forgiven little, loves little." He said to the woman, "Your sins are forgiven." Then those who were at table with him began to say among themselves, "Who is this then who even forgives sins?" And he said to the woman, "Your faith has saved you, go in peace." Luke 7: 36-5

Jimmy Stewart was always one of my favorite actors. Perhaps you remember him from early in his career, *Mr. Smith Goes to Washington*. Remember Mr. Smith? And every holiday season we see Jimmy Stewart as George in *It's a Wonderful Life*. Jimmy made some great westerns, a few comedies, and starred in some of those great Alfred Hitchcock films. Jimmy Stewart. One of my favorites is a little-known film from the 1950's or early 60's, I think, in which Jimmy Stewart plays an aeronautical engineer. He stars with the British actress, Glynis Johns. Jimmy is part of the design team for a new transatlantic airplane, but in the midst of the process Jimmy realizes that this plane is not sound.

In fact, he comes to believe that the wings are going to fall off this plane not long after it takes flight. Of course he warns his superiors in the company and of course they push him aside and ignore him. He makes a big fuss and eventually loses his job; then he gets in trouble with the police because he tries to block the flight.

Who has seen this, who remembers this movie? Anybody? Nobody? Okay. Great movie. (Unfortunately, the title escapes me at the moment.) Eventually the plane is built and makes a successful transatlantic flight with Jimmy aboard! So, it looks like Jimmy the aeronautical engineer has somehow made a mistake in his calculations. The plane lands at Heathrow Airport, passengers disembark and gather in the terminal, where the plane can be seen through the terminal windows. Did I mention that the plane, at rest on the runway, can be seen through the terminal windows? The plane looks fine after that long ocean crossing. Doesn't it look fine to you? No probl....!@#$%!

Jimmy Stewart grew up in Indiana, Pennsylvania. At the 8:30 service, we had two different families who knew the Stewart family and remembered them well. They knew Jimmy's sister and attended the Presbyterian Church where Jimmy's father was the choir director. Jimmy Stewart's father had a hardware store in downtown Indiana. When Jimmy was about 12-years old, the family got a new puppy, but the puppy got loose and was out in the neighborhood. Sadly, another dog in the neighborhood found the puppy and killed it. So Jimmy storms into the hardware store, crying, sad, you know, but also angry. He was so angry that this neighbor dog would kill their new puppy. He tells his father that he could just kill this other dog. His father listens for a moment, then turns and goes to the hardware store's gun rack. He takes down a .22 rifle, opens the bolt, puts in a shell, and hands it to Jimmy. "If you think that is what needs to be done, then do what you think is right," his father says.

So Jimmy takes the gun and goes outside. He doesn't have any trouble finding the dog. The dog is friendly; it wasn't a mean dog. So he puts a leash on the dog and takes it into the alley, ties the dog to a pole, and takes aim. But before Jimmy can pull the trigger, the dog wags his tail! Jimmy can't do it. He couldn't do it. So, he, you know, he unties the dog and lets him go, takes the rifle back to his father, and that's the end of the story. Jimmy's father was obviously a man of considerable wisdom.

That's forgiveness. It's forgiveness. Jimmy could have given the dog, the offending dog, could have given back what he had received, a life for a life, a death for a death; but he didn't. He didn't. He didn't give back the hurt he had received. It's forgiveness. In our English language, the little prefix *for* is often used to mean *not*. If you forgo your vacation, you do *not* go. If you forbid people to come in your door, you do *not* bid them to come in. If you bid them to come in, they will come in, but if you *forbid* them, you tell them not to come in. If I *forget* something, I have sent my memory on an errand to get something but my memory can't find it, does *not get* it for me.

So when you *forgive*, you simply do *not give* back the wound or the hurt that you received. You could choose to give back the harm you received, an eye for an eye, a tooth for a tooth. If someone scratches your car door, I suppose you could bang your car door against that other car door and give him a scratch too. But then your car door would be worse. But if you don't, if you don't give back the scratch you have received, that qualifies as forgiving. *Not giving*.

We have this idea in our society that forgiveness has to do with how you *feel* toward the one who has hurt you. Shouldn't you feel warm and loving toward those who have hurt you? Shouldn't you, you know, forget it? "It's alright; never mind; forget it." Forgiveness has nothing to do with how you feel! You can forgive people that you dislike and intend to continue to dislike. If you don't give back to them the hurt that they have given you, you are technically forgiving them.

So, that sounds pretty easy, doesn't it? Who can forgive? You can forgive. In Ashland, Ohio, the Presbyterian Church has something in its narthex that you don't have here in Winter Haven, Florida. Anybody want to guess what it is? Anyone....? It's called a *coat rack*. All winter long, people come in and hang their coats on it. During one winter, I noticed that a little old lady who was almost always present had been absent for three or four Sundays in a row. I inquired with her friends and they told me that a few weeks earlier someone had taken her coat from the coat rack, and she won't come to a church where they steal your coat. So, I called Mrs. Coatless. I told her how sorry we were that her coat had gotten lost and that we would surely watch for her coat when someone realized the mistake and returned her coat. Eventually she did return to worship; I think it was actually in the spring after the weather got warmer. I didn't say to her what I really wanted to say to her. I was too many years away from retirement to tell her what I really wanted to tell her. I wanted to say to her, "Here is what you should do: come to church next Sunday, and when the congregation starts to sing the last hymn, get up from your pew and go back to the coat rack. Try on coats until you find one that you like, then take it and go home. And I'm sure that whoever's coat you take will forgive you. That person will think it was an innocent mistake."

Of course I didn't say that. But if you do *not take* somebody else's coat after your coat has disappeared, you have exercised forgiveness. You have not given back the harm you suffered. So, if you are worried about forgiving people, this is probably pretty good news. What you have to do to qualify as a forgiver is simply choose not to return the hurt you have received!

That's the good news. Here's the hard news. Forgiving is only the beginning of what God calls us to do! God calls us to be reconciled to one another! Forgive? Yes, of course. Then build bridges, make peace, put aside bitterness, and overcome evil with good. The word the Bible often uses for all of this is *reconciliation*. Be reconciled to the person who has hurt you.

And now we're in deep water. That's why I love this story about the dinner party at the house of Simon the Pharisee. Last Sunday we talked about social conventions surrounding the serving of food. Remember? Nobody serves mashed potatoes for breakfast. You probably have never been to a dinner party in which half of the guests were served on china with silverware and the other half of the guests were served on paper plates with plastic spoons and forks. Anybody ever been to a dinner party like that? No. It would be fun though wouldn't it, to observe people's reactions? We have these conventions, expectations surrounding the eating and serving of food.

It was true in Jesus' day as well. When the guests arrived at the home where the dinner would be served, the host would provide, out on the front porch, a basin of water. The guest would come in off the road. The road was not only dusty, but sometimes there were other things on the road, you know, cows and sheep. You get the picture. So you had a basin to wash your feet on the front porch. (I'm relying here on Dr. Kenneth Bailey's superb work in his study of the parables, *Through Peasant Eyes*.) Next, the host's servant would offer to pour a perfumed ointment, oil, onto your hands; you might rub it on your face or into your hair. Finally, as you arrived at the door, your host would welcome you with a kiss. If the host thought you were more or less his equal in the culture, he would kiss you on the cheek, and you would kiss the host on the cheek. But if the host recognized that you were an honored guest, the host might take your hand and kiss your hand. And if your host recognized you as a rabbi or a teacher or someone of great honor, the host would humble himself, kneel, and kiss your feet. When he arose, he might say, "My house is honored by your presence; please come in."

When Jesus arrives at Simon's house, there is no water. There is no ointment. There is no kiss. But there is a woman who comes in off the street. Luke identifies her as "a woman of the city." We have phrases like that too. It implies a woman of ill repute, though we don't know what her circumstances were. In that culture, any woman out in public without a man was under suspicion. But she shows up at the dinner party, obviously uninvited. She stands weeping at Jesus' feet. Her tears fall upon his feet. She kneels to wipe his feet with her hair. She kisses his feet.

In our culture we have this very old phrase indicating a gesture of vulnerability and self-disclosure. Go ahead, someone say it for us … Yes, thank you. She "let her hair down." Dr. Bailey reminds us that in the Palestinian culture of Jesus' day, a woman would never unfurl her hair except, perhaps, in the darkness and privacy of her bedchamber, but never on any other occasion. But this woman lets her hair down in public to wipe Jesus' feet! It is a moment of extraordinary tenderness and vulnerability. But Simon says, "Don't you know what kind of woman this is?" Actually, that's not quite what he said, because he won't even speak directly to our Lord. He won't even address Jesus personally. He says, "Doesn't *he* know what kind of woman this is?"

Did you see the flash of lightening there? Did you hear the clap of thunder? Did you see the look on our Lord's face as Simon insults this woman in this moment of her helplessness? Gentle Jesus, meek and mild? You think? Simon has just poked a stick in a hornet's nest, and he's about to be stung. "Simon," Jesus says, "I have something to say to you."

And here is the brief parable. A certain creditor had two debtors. One owed $500 and the other owed $50. When they could not pay, the master forgave them both. Which one, do you suppose, will love him more? Simon can see the trap closing around him now. "The one, I suppose, to whom he forgave more," he answered. Jesus said, "You are right."

Then, turning toward the woman, he asks Simon, "Do you see this woman?" Do you *see* her? No. He sees only his own self-righteousness. Simon is a Pharisee and therefore presumably a spiritual leader for God's people. And here is a woman in the most tender and earnest moment of repentance, humbly seeking the mercy of God. And Simon can't see her! But Jesus sees her. "Her sins, which were many, are forgiven; therefore she loved much. But the one who is forgiven little, loves little."

But the thing that is striking about this story is not just that Jesus forgives the woman. And it is not even that Jesus implicitly offers forgiveness to Simon. Simon apparently won't receive it, but the offer is there. What is remarkable here is that Jesus sets forth the terms -- stay with me -- sets forth the terms under which reconciliation can happen.

Reconciliation doesn't mean you have to be the doormat and just keep forgiving and forgiving while someone else keeps piling on the hurt, time after time after time. You can forgive someone whether they are sorry or not. But if you are working at being reconciled to someone, there has to be change. There has to be movement, probably on both sides. You have to say to the other, "Now you've hurt me, and this is how you've hurt me, and I don't want you to hurt me again." And the other person can say the same to you if they wish. Jesus said, "Simon, I came to your house; you gave me no water. She has wet my feet with her tears. You gave me no ointment; she has anointed my feet. You gave me no kiss; she has kissed my feet." This is not Jesus complaining about being slighted by Simon; it is Jesus setting forth the terms by which he and Simon could conceivably be reconciled.

You can always forgive. It's not easy! But it is up to you. But you can't always, by yourself alone, be reconciled, because that depends on the other person too. The other person has to be involved in the reconciliation.

Because this woman is a child of God and a member of the family of God, she has a right to be treated with dignity, to be honored, to be respected as a human being. And you have that right too. You can't always be reconciled with those who have hurt you. All that Jesus asks is that you give it a try.

Let us pray.

Loving God we thank you for the forgiveness you have so generously and freely poured out upon us. Enable us, forgiven, to be forgiving. In Jesus Christ. Amen.

In Everything Give Thanks?

And we exhort you, brothers, and sisters, admonish the idle, encourage the fainthearted, help the weak, be patient with them all. See that none of you repays evil for evil, but always seek to do good to one another and to all. Rejoice always, pray constantly, in everything give thanks; for this is the will of God in Christ Jesus for you. I Thessalonians 5: 14-18

I had to get my glasses adjusted this week. When I would get out of the car here in the parking lot each morning on my way into the office, within two or three seconds I would lose sight in my left eye. This concerned me. Then I realized that as I went from the air-conditioned car to the moist morning air, my lenses were fogging up. But only the left lens! Upon closer examination, I realized that the frames of my glasses were badly bent, thrusting the left lens tight against my face with no room for ventilation, while the right lens was so far from my face that it was a wonder I could see at all. So I needed an adjustment.

I passed the optometrist's office several times, thinking that I'd do it later when I wasn't so busy. But Friday, on the way home from a hospital call, I finally made myself stop. Of course there were several people ahead of me, so I had to wait a while, which was fine, but the whole thing was kind of a nuisance. But they're fixed; now I can see again.

While that was happening this week, I was of course preparing this sermon and reflecting on the Apostle Paul's charge to the church in Thessalonica. He said, "In everything give thanks." And I realized that I hadn't really followed that admonition very well in the matter of bent glasses. In everything give thanks. How do you do that? I wanted to ask Paul what he meant by that and how in the world one does it.

So I sent him an email. I posed questions; he replied. Actually we had quite a lively conversation. And this morning I want to tell you how it went.

First, I said, "Paul, I'd like to ask you some questions about your first letter to the Thessalonians."

He said, "What part?"

I said, "Chapter five."

He said, "You want to ask me about my list of instructions to the church."

I said, "That's right."

Well at that point Paul more or less took over the conversation. He said, "Do you follow my instructions?"

"I try," I answered.

"Do you admonish the unruly?" he asked.

"Every Sunday morning," I said.

"Do you support the weak?"

"I try to encourage both the weak and the strong; we have a lot of strong folks in our congregation," I answered.

"I like that," Paul said. "That's good. Do you return no one evil for evil?"

"That's a hard one," I said.

"Well what's the problem then?" he asked.

"Well it's this business about giving thanks in everything." Then I told him about my problem with the bent glasses and how I didn't really do very well in giving thanks in that situation.

So Paul said to me, "Do you have glasses?"

"Yes, I do," I said.

"I didn't," he said. And that reminded me that Paul had problems with his eyesight and that it was a serious impediment to his ministry. "I didn't have glasses," he repeated. "You have glasses. Are you thankful or your glasses?"

"Yes, of course I am," I said.

"And do you have a good eye doctor that you can go to whenever you have a problem? "he asked. "And are you thankful for that?"

"Yes," I answered. "Our Dr. Henne is excellent; he is always there when we need him. We are indeed thankful for his care."

Paul continued, "And when you get home with your glasses, will you have books to read? And newspapers? And magazines? And a Bible? Large print if you need it." Paul wasn't finished. "Does your Bible have *pages* to turn? Do you know how hard it is to read the verse you want when you have to unroll a scroll to find it?"

I was starting to regret that I had raised the issue of my bent glasses. But Paul still wasn't finished. "You have a lot of sunlight there in central Florida; you can read all day long if you want to. And you have electric lights, so you can read far into the night. Are you thankful for that?"

"Yes, of course," I said

I could hardly slow him down now. "Faces," he said. "Can you see faces with those glasses? Faces of your loved ones, faces of your friends? Can you see their smiles and their occasional tears? Can you see the unfathomable mystery of the human face? Are you thankful for that?"

"Yes," I said.

"And what about colors? Can you see colors? Blue sky? Golden leaves in the autumn? Red apples ripening in the sun? Are you thankful for colors?"

"Yes," I said. "I'm beginning to get your point, sir."

"Okay," he said. "Anything else?"

"Just this." I said. "This idea of giving thanks *in everything* is hard to preach. We have some people in our congregation who are going through some pretty hard times right now. There are folks struggling to make it through the storm. We've had a lot of sadness here this year; there are more than a few homes in this community where there will be an empty chair at the table when the family gathers for the holidays this year. Can I say to people, 'In everything give thanks?' It's hard."

"I know it's hard," Paul answered. "But study Thessalonica."

"You mean the book," I asked.

"No," he said. "The city."

"I'm not sure I understand what you mean," I said. I told him that I have studied the city of Thessalonica a bit. I know it was a little town on the southern coast of Greece; the town was in ancient times known as *Thermae* because there are hot springs there. *Thermae* is the Greek word for hot springs. From that Greek word we get our words *thermal, thermos, thermometer, thermostat*. But I didn't think that's what Paul meant. So I said, "Paul, I know that in 314 B.C.E. Thermae was conquered by the Greek general Cassander, who remodeled the city, built temples and roads and public spaces so that it became one of the loveliest cities of the ancient world. Then he renamed it after his wife Thessa. That's how it became *Thessalonica*. And that would be only moderately interesting except for the fact that Thessa was the daughter of Philip of Macedon, famed conqueror of most of the Mediterranean world. And Philip of Macedon was the father of Alexander the Great! So Thessa and Alexander were half-brother and sister." So I said to Paul, "Is that what we should study? Is that what you want us to know about Thessalonica?"

And Paul said, "No. No. No. Don't waste your congregation's time with that dusty old history!"

"What then?" I said.

And he said, "Study Thessalonica." Then he signed off.

So I thought I had better take one more look at Thessalonica. This is what I found, and then we'll be done. Thessalonica was the first city on the continent of Europe that the Apostle Paul visited. He was there long before he ever got to Rome. So his arrival in Thessalonica represented the taking of the Gospel to a whole new continent.

And here's what happened there when Paul arrived. It's all described in Acts, chapter 17. Paul went straight to the synagogue and began to teach. Three Sabbaths in a row, three weeks, he shared the Good News of Jesus in the synagogue. And after three weeks, the leaders of the synagogue were so angry with Paul that they went out into the streets, gathered up a mob, and began to hunt him down. First, they went to the house of Jason, where Paul was staying. They arrested Jason, dragged him through the streets, and threw him in jail. But Paul had just left the house, so they continued to search for him. Paul and his companion Silas hid themselves until nightfall. Then under the cover of darkness, Paul's few friends there smuggled him out of the city, and he and Silas escaped.

That's what happened in Thessalonica. He was there only three weeks, and by all human standards it was a total disaster from which he barely escaped with his life. Complete failure, or so it appeared.

But a tiny community of faith survived there, just a handful of brave souls. They endured the animosity of their neighbors. But over time, the Thessalonian Church, not more than a dozen or so in number at first, began to grow. Soon they were sharing their faith with other towns and peoples in Greece and beyond. You've heard of the Greek Orthodox Church. And the Russian Orthodox Church. And the Roman Catholic Church. And the Protestant Churches.

You've heard of St. Francis and Joan of Arc. You've heard of Martin Luther, John Calvin, and John Knox. These towering figures and the Christian communities they represent are arguably the spiritual legacy of Paul's "failed" ministry in Thessalonica. If you would take a map of Europe and trace the movements of the Gospel message, those paths would all begin in Thessalonica. But they would take you to the most remote corners of Europe, eventually crossing seas and oceans, bringing the Gospel to New Worlds. This is the spiritual legacy of Paul's disastrous three weeks in Thessalonica.

In everything give thanks. Maybe what Paul meant was that you never know how things are going to turn out when God is involved. So give thanks.

And it is interesting to me that the best evidence suggests that this letter to the Thessalonian Church may very well have been the first book of our New Testament ever written. Years before the four Gospels were written, or any others of the letters in our Bible, this letter was on its way to Paul's friends in Thessalonica. And when Paul put his primitive pen to parchment, straining to see the letters his own hand had written, he could hardly have known how far his words would travel, how long they would be cherished, and how many souls would take heart in reading them.

In everything, yes everything, give thanks.

Let us pray.

Loving God, inspire us by the example of those who have been faithful across the years, and enable us to be faithful in sharing your love in the years you have given us. In Jesus Christ. Amen

A Doll, A Plastic Cow, And A Painting

One of the two who heard John speak and followed him was Andrew, Simon Peter's brother. He first found his brother Simon and said to him, "We have found Messiah" (which means Christ). He brought him to Jesus. Jesus looked at him and said, "So you are Simon, the son of John? You shall be called Cephas" (which means Peter).

The next day, Jesus decided to go to Galilee. And he found Philip and said to him, "Follow me." Now Philip was from Bethsaida, the city of Andrew and Peter. Philip found Nathaniel and said to him, "We have found him of whom Moses and also the prophets wrote, Jesus of Nazareth, the son of Joseph." John 1:40-45

Do you ever watch the *Antiques Roadshow*? No, it's not a show about when the preacher and his wife go on vacation. The *Antiques Roadshow* calls together a traveling group of appraisers in the field of antiques, and people bring in their family treasures to be identified and appraised. So if you found a box of old photographs in the attic, or a box of sheet music, or a vase, or a ring, or a sword, or.... (you get the idea). What do you have? Is it an Ansel Adams photograph? Is it an Abraham Lincoln signature? Is it a Tiffany vase? Sometimes the family treasure turns out to be genuinely valuable, and sometimes its value turns out to be primarily sentimental.

If you followed the news this week you may have heard a story very much like what happens on the *Roadshow*. A couple of years ago a woman in West Virginia bought a box of junk at a flea market. She took it home and, without much fanfare, shoved it into a closet for two years. But her family got to suggesting that she have it looked at. Now the box included a baby doll, a plastic toy cow, and a painting in a frame. And on the front of the frame was a plaque with one word: *Renoir*. But many paintings claim to be *Renoir*, you know, so she didn't think much about it at the time. But she took it to an appraiser. Her painting was, she was told, a legitimate work of art painted by the French Impressionist Pierre-Auguste Renoir! And the appraiser told her that it could be worth $100,000! She paid $7 for the box. Well, that's a pretty good return on investment.

So the auction to sell her painting was scheduled for last week. But at the last moment the auction was postponed because it was discovered that this painting had been *stolen* from the Baltimore Museum of Art in 1951. It has been missing for over 60 years. The investigation also showed that an insurance company had paid the Baltimore Museum of Art $2500 in 1951 to settle its claim for the lost painting. So the insurance company thinks the painting belongs to them. They paid for it. The Baltimore Museum of Art thinks the painting belongs to them. And of course the lady who found it in a box of junk thinks that she has a claim to the painting. So here's how the story ends.... I have no idea how it will end. Many months of negotiations will ensue, and I will report back to you if I learn the outcome.

If you could see the painting in person, you might understand how it got pushed to the back of the closet. Now maybe I am going to reveal my vast field of ignorance about art in the next few minutes. But to me, it's not what you call a pretty picture. It's French Impressionism, a school of art that followed Realism and preceded Cubism. Picasso was a Cubist. But for about 30 years, 1880-1910, Impressionism was all the rage in art. The Impressionists used bold brushstrokes, bold colors, straight out of the tube, no blending to get muted or subtle colors. Take a streak of white, and a streak of red, and a streak of orange side by side, unmixed, unblended, bold. The Realists had been trying to paint what you actually see. They tried to paint nature and reality just as your eye would see it. The Impressionists said, "No, no, no. That's not how you paint. You paid for the *impression* of reality. Paint what you would see at a glance." The title of this particular Renoir painting translates to "Landscape on the Banks of the Seine." But if you could see a river, or the banks of a river, well, congratulations.

Impressionism paved the way for the painters whose names most of us recognize Cezanne, Gauguin, Van Gogh. They were all Post-Impressionists; they used even bolder colors and even bolder strokes. And so Renoir opened the door to a whole new chapter in the history of art.

Now some of you are accomplished painters; I've seen your canvases. Some of you could paint a pretty good copy of "Landscape on the Banks of the Seine." If you worked at it a while, you could copy this painting, brushstroke by brushstroke. I think you could do it. But even if you could make a perfect copy of Renoir's painting, I'm sorry to tell you that your copy wouldn't be worth $100,000, because it wasn't Renoir that painted it. The value of a piece of art is directly related to the person who creates it. The value of this painting is not that it is so beautiful, though if you loved Impressionist art, maybe you would think it a masterpiece. The value of this painting is that it comes from the hand of Auguste Renoir.

Renoir was a hero and an inspiration to many people. In the last years of his life as an artist, he suffered from arthritis in both hands. At the end, he had his assistants strap his brushes to his curled hands so that he could continue to paint the things he loved. His life was an inspiration. The value of the painting is related inevitably and inseparably to the person who painted it.

And isn't that true for many of the things we cherish? Think about the things you own that you wouldn't sell for any price: your grandmother's wedding ring; or a photograph of your parents on the day of their wedding; or the rusty old tools from the family farm that your grandparents used in New York or Ohio or Indiana a century ago; a pocket watch, perhaps; or the flag your daddy brought home after his term of military service overseas. Or the family Bible. The things that you cannot put a price on are priceless to you because of the people whose hands once held them. These objects are treasures to you because the people they represent are treasures to you.

May I ask you to think for a moment about the people who have been treasures in your life? Your mother and father? Grandparents? A teacher who inspired you? A coach who believed in you? A friend who stood by you in a moment of need? Your brother? Your sister? We thank God when we have found such treasure!

That's why I chose today's scripture passage. As I read these verses this week, I was surprised. I had never noticed before how many times in this little story we hear the word *found*. Andrew *found* his brother Simon

Peter. Now we talked about brothers last week. Jacob and Esau, Cain and Able: they had very troubled relationships. Those brothers were truly *lost* to one another. That's not what is happening here. Simon Peter wasn't lost. He wasn't lost in any sense. He just wasn't with Andrew at that particular moment. So, what a strange word to use: *found*. Andrew found his brother. He wasn't lost, but he found him. I think it means that he connected with him in a new way. He said, "Pete, Pete, come over here; you've got to see this. Pete, you need to meet this person."

Andrew found his brother. Then as we read on, Jesus went to Galilee and *found* Philip. Philip wasn't lost; but Jesus found him, connected with him in a new way. Then Philip went out and *found* Nathaniel. Nathaniel wasn't lost; he just wasn't present. But Philip found him, connected with him in a new way.

Sometimes those who are closest to us, those who are right beside us, get lost. Not in the sense that the prodigal son got lost or Jacob and Esau got lost but lost in the busy-ness of life. Amidst the press of the responsibilities of daily living, those who are our true treasures sometimes get pushed to the back of the closet, so to speak. And from time to time, we have to *find* one another. You may have to make an appointment or at least try to find the one who has drifted away. I think that is part of what is going on in these verses. The first thing Andrew wanted to do after he found Jesus, was to find his brother Simon.

Of course, like the woman who bought the Renoir, we don't always recognize our treasures as treasures until some time has passed. Sometimes we don't recognize at the time how profoundly important someone has been to our subsequent happiness or success. How do you measure treasure? The Halls of Fame in every sport contain more than a few champions who, at the beginning of their careers, were not stars. No one noticed them particularly. They seemed at first to be more or less average players. They got to the Halls of Fame because, year after year after year, you could count on them, the team could depend on them to be at their best when they were needed most. They were not spectacular stars at the beginning, but year after year they were reliable, dependable, just like the people you cherish.

Aren't You Glad You're Here This Morning?

In the church I served in Ohio, one of our elders brought me a cartoon one day. He had cut it out of a magazine; he thought it was so funny. The cartoon depicted a man seated behind a desk in an office. The only unusual thing about the scene was that there was a big nameplate on the desk, and it was blank. So here's a man working at a desk, but his nameplate is empty. And off to one side of the cartoon there are two men standing outside the office door pointing in at the man behind the desk. One of them says to the other, "McGrath has been with the company ten years, but he still hasn't made a name for himself." That's why he brought me the cartoon. He thought it was so funny.

Lots of folks go unnoticed at first, but years later, you recognize that that friend, that neighbor, that teacher, was a real treasure for you. Years later sometimes. We got word this week that Dr. Gabriel Vahanian died at age 85 in his home in Strasbourg, France. Dr. Vahanian was a professor of theology for more than 30 years at Syracuse University in New York. He wrote a little book in 1960 in which he was the first to use the phrase, "the death of God." And some of you will remember hearing about a theological movement called the Death of God Theology. It was written up in *Time* magazine and many other periodicals. But the popular reporting never fully understood what Dr. Vahanian and those who followed him were talking about. He didn't mean that *God* had died; that would be ridiculous. What he was trying to say was that the culture in which we live no longer is able to experience God. The culture's ability to experience and talk about and think about God is what has actually withered and died. It was a very important theological insight. And indeed it changed the world of 20th century theology.

Well, after his time at Syracuse, Dr. Vahanian went back to his native France. He was appointed to the Chair of Theology at the University of Strasbourg, which is widely recognized as the most prestigious Protestant Chair of Theology in all of France. So his work was acclaimed all over France and all over Europe. And he had many friends and admirers in the United States. In fact, he had friends in Winter Haven. Each year, when he vacationed from his teaching, he would come to Winter Haven. And when he came to Winter Haven, he worshipped Sunday after Sunday here at our church. Some of you will remember him. He sat right out here, had a cane, and I think it is accurate to say he was the only man in 20 years who has come to this church in a three-piece suit, white shirt, and tie.

And he came year after year, and Sunday after Sunday, treasure right here in our midst. He never said what he thought of the sermons. But I know how much he appreciated our organist and our choir because I could see it in his face as he worshipped. One Sunday, when I anticipated that he would be here, I deliberately included in my sermon a passage from one of his books and quoted him by name. When he came out the door, he shook my hand, and with the faintest smile on his face, said to me, "You read good books."

Who knew? World famous theologian here with you at this church. I sent our sympathy to his family. We shall miss him. I shall miss him.

Our treasures sometimes go unnoticed. But Andrew found his brother Peter. Philip found his friend Nathaniel. And together they found Messiah, who is, after all, the greatest treasure you can ever find.

Let us pray.

Loving God, with grateful hearts we remember those who have helped us along the way. Let us cherish them as you have cherished us in Christ Jesus. Amen.

Bermuda Bay

And God said to Elijah, "Go forth and stand upon the mountain before the Lord." And behold, the Lord passed by, and a great and strong wind rent the mountains and broke in pieces the rocks before the Lord. But the Lord was not in the wind. And after the wind, an earthquake. But the Lord was not in the earthquake. And after the earthquake, a fire. But the Lord was not in the fire. And after the fire, a still, small voice. I Kings 19: 11-12

What we're going to talk about today is the character of God. The Bible is not an easy book to read. If you have tried to read the Bible, you have come upon some stories that are difficult to understand, far removed from our experience. But it always helps, it seems to me, to ask the question, "What does this story tell us about the character of God?" Indeed, I think this is how Jesus read his Bible. If I had the time, and I'm not going to take the time this morning, but if I took the time, I think I could persuade you that this is how Jesus in fact read his Bible. He asked the question, "What does this tell us about the character of God?"

If you've been around the church very long, you've heard this text: There was a great wind. God was not in the wind. There was a great earthquake. God was not in the earthquake. There was a great fire. God was not in the fire. And then there was a still small voice. Elijah heard God in that still small voice. What does that tell us about the character of God? That's what we're going to talk about this morning.

On Saturdays, I always try to read the church page in the local newspaper. I like to read the advertisements for other churches in our community to see if there's someplace I'd rather attend. So far there's not. But this caught my eye not long ago. One of our local churches advertises itself in this way: "We are receiving the truth, not criticizing it. We are declaring the truth, not merely discussing it." Isn't that fun? Elijah would love that church. We are declaring the truth, not merely discussing it!

Elijah was a no-nonsense, no-compromise person and prophet. And so it troubled Elijah greatly that in his day, in the nation of Israel, people were worshipping two gods. Some people were worshipping the god of Israel, Yahweh. Other people were worshipping this other god, Baal. And some people were hedging their bets and worshipping both. So if you walked down the street in Elijah's time, here is the First Church of Yahweh on one corner, and across the street, the First Church of Baal. And lots of people worshipped Baal, including Israel's queen, Jezebel. And this was greatly troubling to Elijah. When he could stand it no longer, he called in the priests of Baal and said, "Let's have a contest. Let's have a showdown and we'll find out once and for all whose god is God." And the priests of Baal said, "That's fine."

So this is what they did. And again, if you've been around the church for a while, you know this story. Elijah said, "We'll both build altars, and we'll both pile them up with wood, and we'll both take oxen and cut them into pieces and put them on the wood. And then, we'll pray to our respective gods to light the fire, and we'll see whose fire gets lit and whose sacrifice gets offered." And the priests of Baal said, "That sounds good to us. We'll do it." Elijah said, "You go first."

So about nine o'clock in the morning the priests of Baal started. They built their altar out of stones and piled it up with wood and cut up their ox and put it on the wood. And all morning long they danced around the altar and prayed and chanted. And nothing happened. And about lunchtime they took a break. Then they resumed after lunch. When they got into their most extreme frenzy, they began to cut themselves with knives as was the custom. They cut their chests and the tops of their heads, and blood dripped down on their white robes. What a spectacle! And nothing happened.

All this time Elijah (who wasn't really a very nice person in some ways) was standing at the edge of the crowd taunting them. Taunting them! You can read this in the story -- it's in the 18th chapter. Taunting. "Hey! Whoa! What's happening? Where's your god now? Is your god on vacation? Oh, your god must've taken a nap this afternoon!" He's taunting them all afternoon. And about four o'clock, when they'd danced until they could dance no more, they gave up. The priests of Baal said "All right, Mr. Smarty. It's your turn."

So Elijah builds an altar, piles it with wood, puts on the ox. And they said, "Are you ready?" And he said, "No. There's going to be a big fire here, so you'd better call up the volunteer fire department." This is all in there, in the chapter. You can read it. And so they went down to the village spring and filled their buckets and returned. And Elijah said, "All right, now pour the water on the wood. Pour the water on the altar, on the ox. Dig a trench around this altar and fill it up with water." And they did. And they said, "All right, all right. Are you ready?" And he said, "No. Do it again." And so they did it all over again. "Are you ready?" "No, do it again." So they did it three times. It's all there in the Bible; you'll want to read this story yourself in chapter 18.

You know what's coming.

"Are you ready yet?" "Yeah, I'm ready." And Elijah bowed his head and prayed and no sooner had his prayer ended, then...you know. BOOM!

A flash of lightning hit that altar dead center, vaporized the ox, vaporized the wood, vaporized the altar, vaporized the water in the ditch around it. Singed everybody's eyebrows. Clap of thunder. Great victory. Elijah's God wins.

But that's not quite the end. Elijah, filled with adrenaline, just full of himself and this great victory, goes off-script. God didn't tell him to do what he did next. There's no record in the story that God ordered this, but Elijah was very excited. He pulled out his sword and began to hack away at the priests of Baal. Just hacked away at them. And of course, the onlookers--everybody wants to be on the winning side, you know-- the onlookers took out their swords and they began to slaughter the priests of Baal. And that day they slaughtered 450 of the priests of Baal. God didn't tell them to do that, as far as the record shows. But that's what they did.

Well, when Jezebel found out that 450 of her favorite pastors had been slain, she fired off an angry email to Elijah that said, in effect, "I hope you enjoy supper tonight, because it'll be your last. I'm going to get you." And then the story takes a curious turn.

You might expect Elijah to say, "Well, bring it on! Come and get me! You know where I am. The mighty God is with me. I'm not afraid of you." But that's not what happened. The adrenaline has begun to wear off, and Elijah realizes that his physical life is in danger. And so he runs out of the city, down the road, out into the wilderness, hides in a cave and falls asleep. That's Elijah the brave prophet.

Well, in many ways this is the best part of the story. Because even though Elijah is discouraged and afraid, God comes to him. God ministers to him in the very moment of his need. God sends an angel, bakes him a cake, gives him a pitcher of water to refresh him. Elijah wakes up, eats the cake—do you know what kind of cake it was? Yes, thank you, it was angel food cake, of course. But Elijah is still discouraged and so God comes to him. And God calls him out of the cave and says, "Come on out here, come on up to this mountain top. I'm going to show you something." There is a mighty wind, so mighty that it pulls the stones off the face of the rock cliffs. There is an earthquake and a fire. But God is not in the wind. God is not in the earthquake. God is not in the fire. God is in the quiet voice of assurance that comes to Elijah out of the darkness of the cave and the stillness of Elijah's need.

What does this tell us about the character of God? It tells us that sometimes God is subtle. Sometimes God is gentle, tender. Quite often in fact, God whispers. Moses had the same experience when he received the Ten Commandments. You remember the story? Moses says to God, "Show me your glory, so I'll know where these commandments are coming from." And God answers him, "No mortal man can see my glory and live. I have to cover myself with a veil or you'd be blown away." God accommodates God's-self to the circumstances of our humanity. Can I say that again? God accommodates God's-self to us in our humanity.

What does lightning do to the circuitry of your television or your computer? It blows it out. God accommodates God's-self to us. If you think about the Christian message, this accommodation is everywhere in the story. Think about Christmas. How does the mighty God send God's son into the world? A peasant girl gives birth to a child and lays him on a bed of straw. Hallelujah! God has entered human life. Quietly, tenderly. Think about Easter's great celebration of Christ's victory. How does Easter morning unfold? With trumpets, with a parade? No, but with the silence of an early morning in the garden, and the quietness of an empty tomb.

Think about your own experience, when you have felt the nearness, the presence of God. It may have been in an earthquake, wind, or fire. Maybe. Some people have those experiences. Dramatic, emotional experiences, that's fine. But I think most of us experience God in the quietness of a note from a friend in a time of your sorrow. Or in the joy of seeing your grandchildren. Or your great-grandchildren! How amazing! A sunset. The melody of a song remembered from long ago. The fellowship of your family table at Thanksgiving or at Christmas. God comes to us sometimes subtly, quietly, in a still, small voice. Listen. Listen.

I painted my front door this week. It had been a kind of maroon red color, but my front door is set back in a little alcove. It's recessed into the front of the house, and so it's always in shadows, where the front door more or less disappeared. It just didn't make any kind of a statement at all. So I said to my wife, "I'm a little tired of the dark red color. I'd like to paint the front door." And she said, "You know, I've been thinking about that too." I said, "So what color should we paint it?" And she said, "Well, I saw on one of those shows that dark maroon red color is out." No disrespect if you have a red door. But the color that's really in right now, if you really want to be with it, is teal. Teal. Not blue, not green, but teal. Did you know that? Aren't you glad you're here this morning?

So we went down to our favorite paint store and picked out some samples, some paint chips. And we had lots of choices. For example, we could have chosen "Radiant Teal Velveteen," but that was a little strong. "Cool and Clear Turquoise" was nice, but it was a little pale. Then there was "Shimmering Summer Pool." Aren't these names great? Or, I loved this: "Lyric Water Dance." Isn't that great? But our favorite by far, and we both agreed on this, surprisingly, was "Bermuda Bay." Now I've never been to Bermuda, but when I looked at that little three-inch square of color, I could just imagine, you know, the clear waters of the Atlantic washing up on the sand of a Bermuda bay.

So, one evening last week, I painted the front door. And I could tell it was going on a little strong, but you know, when it dries, it darkens down a little. So I painted the front door. I painted the walls around the front door. I painted the side walls of the alcove. And then there was a little trim strip around the outside that I painted. I wanted to make a statement. I wanted people to notice that we'd painted our front door. So, when I got all finished, I stepped back to admire my work. I turned my back to the doorway and walked down the sidewalk a bit, and then deliberately turned around.

My house had disappeared! The door was all that there was! It was as though the center square in Hollywood Squares had gone berserk and eaten all of the other squares, you know? It was just too much. And so I called my wife. She agreed that it was just too strong, too much. But now it's late in the evening, and so we had to leave it until the next day. We both agreed that we had to do something to tone down Bermuda Bay. And I knew for sure we had to do something when at lunchtime the next day, I saw on the news that the FAA, the Federal Aviation Administration, was investigating some reports by pilots that they had been temporarily blinded flying over the city of Winter Haven, Florida.

So the next evening, I got out some beige paint and painted the side walls of the alcove, you know? Painted out the trim and toned it down. But it was still a little strong. And so I thought, "Well, we'll put a wreath on the front door. That will tone it down a bit." Well, a wreath isn't solid; you can see through it. And that Bermuda Bay showed right through the wreath, so that wasn't the answer. So we ended up with a kind of metal art piece that's solid. It blocks out a big portion of the door. So that's where we are right now, and I think it's a little better. Still pretty strong, but it is absolutely the most beautiful door in our neighborhood! There's no question about that.

Isn't that silly? Sometimes less is more. Sometimes subtle is better. God knows that. God accommodates God's-self to us, drawing near in the stillness of our yearning hearts.

Let us pray:

Give us the gift of discernment, O God, that we may see you when you cloth yourself in shadows and hear you when you whisper our names. In Jesus Christ, Amen.

The Ritual Of Artificial Friendship

These things I have spoken to you that my joy may be in you and that your joy may be full. This is my commandment, that you love one another as I have loved you. Greater love has no one than this: that a person lay down his life for his friends. You are my friends if you do what I command you. No longer do I call you servants, for the servant does not know what his master is doing. But I have called you friends, for all that I have heard from my father I have made known to you. You did not choose me, but I chose you. John 15: 11-16

Our scripture lessons this morning presents the words Jesus spoke to the disciples as he ate with them in an upper room the night before his death. If you've been around the church very much at all, you know we have a name for this occasion. We call it the *Last Supper*. I wish we didn't call it the Last Supper. I know this is an argument that I'm probably going to lose, but it seems to me that it is misleading to call it the Last Supper.

The Last Supper suggests to me a time of sadness, parting, farewells. But the conversation at this meal was about joy! Jesus says, "I give you my joy that your joy may be full." It doesn't sound like "Goodbye" to me. If it's a Last Supper, you'd think they would reminisce a while. You know, like, "Hey remember the time that Peter fell out of the boat? Remember the time we caught so many fish that the nets began to break? Remember the time that we fed all those folks from two loaves and five fish? Remember the time we got a flat tire on the way to church? Remember?" You get the idea.

But that's not what's happening at this dinner. The focus on this dinner is not yesterday and the past; the focus is on tomorrow, on the future. Rather than call it the Last Supper, I would like to call it the *Lasting* Supper. It *has* lasted! And every time we gather at this table we reenact and renew and participate in that supper. And in our Presbyterian family of churches, even on those occasions when we don't celebrate the Lord's Supper, we always worship in the *presence* of the Table. The Table is always with us to remind us that this supper lives on. It is the

Lasting Supper. It is in many ways the *first* supper for a new family, the family of Christ's disciples. Our family. Your family.

And it is the occasion when Jesus gives a new commandment. He says, "Love one another." That's not new. That's not the new part. He says, "Love one another *as I have loved you.*" That's the new part. They couldn't know before that night just how he loved them. How much he loved them. But in the 18 hours which would follow this supper, they would learn full well how he loved them as he gave himself on the cross for their sakes. They couldn't know it before. But now that they know how he loves them, maybe they will be more able to love one another. Now. Now their togetherness will embody his love. I worked on that a long time. I'm going to say that again.

Now, at this first and lasting supper, now their togetherness will embody a new understanding of his love. "Love one another," he says, "as I have loved you." And it's not easy. And that's what I want us to think about this morning.

It's not easy to love one another. A few weeks ago on September 11th, we had a guest pastor here. She led you in the Passing of the Peace, the sharing of the peace of Christ in the service. And some of you said to me, "That was different. We liked that." And some of you said to me, "That was different…"

We'll do that again. We used to do that all the time. We used to do it every Sunday. And we listed it in the order of service and called it "The Ritual of Christian Fellowship." Remember that? Who's been around long enough to remember "The Ritual of Christian Fellowship?" We did that. Every Sunday we did that.

And then one Sunday somebody said something to me. I don't know whether what was said was intentional or just accidental. But someone referred to that moment in our service as "The ritual of artificial friendship." And I thought to myself, "Ouch! Is that what it feels like?" So we don't do that as often anymore. I probably shouldn't be telling you all this, but it seems to me that God calls us to more than artificial friendship. God calls us to real caring. We shouldn't have to *script* it. Maybe we ought to let the Spirit move us to pass the peace of Christ to one another spontaneously. And often! Maybe more than once a week!

It's not easy. It's not easy to love one another. Last Sunday afternoon I boarded a flight for Pittsburgh, Pennsylvania, where I have spent the week on study leave. I'll tell you more about that in a minute. One of the women in our class was reflecting on a painful experience she had in her church. She was the pastor, and she was attending a meeting. And one of the folks at the meeting took exception to something that she had done and just unloaded on her, accused her of all kinds of things, and just said the meanest things anyone had ever said to her. And when the meeting ended, this young woman, the pastor, left the meeting very upset, went out into the hallway quite concerned about what had just happened. And she ran smack into one of her colleagues. This colleague recognized that she looked upset, and said to her, "You look like you need a hug. Let me give you a hug."

This pastor said that she reacted to this offer of support in a most unexpected way: she wrapped her own arms tightly around herself and said to her concerned colleague, "Don't touch me! Don't touch me! I don't want to be touched right now. I need some space right now."

When I heard her tell that story, I thought, you know, what a perfectly natural reaction. Sometimes when we love one another, the most loving thing we can do is to back off, give some space. Later, I'm sure she welcomed the hug and the concern of her colleague, but not right then. It's not always easy to know how to love one another.

I learned some things at seminary this week that surprised me. At my alma mater Pittsburgh Theological Seminary, there is no longer a bookstore on campus. Now think about that. There is no bookstore. You go to the bookstore to buy your textbooks and your extra reading, pencils, tablets, papers, you know, whatever you need. There's no longer a bookstore on campus; hundreds of students but no bookstore. The bookstore lost so much money over the last three or four years that they had to close it. Students were buying their books online. Now they have to. The world has changed. No bookstore.

And I knew that there are many more women in ministry than there used to be, many more than when I was in seminary. But I was surprised that in my class of 21 students this week, there were nine men and 12 women. Interesting. And at least half of the pastors who were there were serving churches that had either just merged with another congregation or were about to merge because they were so small, they couldn't survive alone. The pastors of these churches were serving two or more congregations simultaneously. One of the women pastors was serving four congregations at the same time. This reminded me that across the country, our Presbyterian churches are by and large small churches. About 50% of the Presbyterian churches in the country are sufficiently small that they cannot hire a full-time pastor. Did you know that? We are a denomination of small churches. Vital, loving places, good churches, but they're small. So I learned some things and was reminded of some things this week.

At the end of each day's class session we had what was called a Bible study. This is how it went: we went around the room and numbered ourselves. "One, two, three, one, two, three…" And then all the ones went to one room, and all the twos went to another, and all the threes went to another. You've done that, you know. And the leader passed out a long sheet of instructions for the Bible study. One, two, three, four, five, six, seven – a whole page of instructions, handed it to one of us as we went off to our assigned locations to do the Bible study.

So I was numbered one. I went to the room where the ones were, and I entered the room and soon realized I was the only man in that group. There were seven or eight women and me. So that was all right. Then I realized, having spent the day with these people, that I was in a group composed entirely of introverts. Now, you know we call introverted people shy, but that's not really a very accurate way of describing us. We are quiet. We're not the first to speak, you know. Extroverts are more gregarious and have lots to say, but introverts are reserved you might say. And I realized that we had a roomful of quiet people. And then I realized that there was no assigned leader for the Bible study.

So here we are, sitting around the table with this sheet of instructions and Instruction #1 says a person will read the prayer to get this started. So we all sat there shuffling our instruction sheets, but nothing was happening. And I wanted to say, "Hey, let's get started here, I'll do the prayer. It's been a long day, let's get this over with." But I was the only man in the room. And theological seminary today is a very politically correct place, so I wasn't about to assume that I should be the leader. So I sat quietly. And finally, finally, one of the women pastors began to read the prayer and I thought, "Ah, okay, here we go, we're getting on with this." And so we read the prayer, then checked to see what the instructions called for next. Of course, ministers always follow instructions. Step Two said, "Read the Bible passage aloud."

So we read the Bible passage out loud. Next you go around the room and, without discussion, without comment, each person repeats a word or a phrase that they heard in the Bible reading that was especially meaningful. So you just go around the circle and that's pretty easy. We didn't have too much trouble doing that; you just say one word, you know, "bread" or "love" or "forgive," whatever word you want to say.

Next step: read the Bible passage again. Well, oh boy. So, another person eventually starts to read the Bible passage. Then you go around the circle again and say another word that's meaningful to you. And then, do it a third time – read the Bible passage, go around the circle, say a word, etc. Then, according to the instructions, each person is to say what you hear God calling you personally to do in this Bible passage. Now that was harder, because that meant we had to reveal something about ourselves, to share something about ourselves. But we managed that. We got around the circle. Everybody had a little something to say. Nobody comments on the other person's contributions. You just say what God is calling you to do. All right, we're getting toward the bottom of the page now, and we come to the last instruction.

Last instruction: "Bow your head and pray aloud for the person on your right." Out loud! Pray for this person who is a virtual stranger. You may not even know their names. Fortunately, we had name tags, you know, but we hadn't all learned everybody's names. So you're praying out loud for this stranger. And that means that the person on your left is soon going to pray for *you* out loud. And in the group of introverts assembled there, this was painful! This was so far outside our collective comfort zone that I thought the paint was going to peel off the walls of that room. I mean, you could feel how hard this was for us. And what made it worse was that we knew we'd have to come back the next day and the next day and the next day and do it all again! It was just so painful. It got easier. I mean, it didn't ever get easy, but we got a little more comfortable with each other as the week went by.

But in the midst of that, I had a moment of clarity. What must it feel like to visit a church for the first time, to visit a place where you don't know anybody? How threatening that must be to folks, especially to folks who may lean toward an introverted approach to public relationships. How difficult it must be. Maybe the pastor will ask me to stand up and say something or confess my sins or say a prayer or something. You know, I bet there are literally millions of people who stay away from church because they're not sure what's going to happen to them when they get here. They've heard stories or seen movies; they don't know how uncomfortable it's going to be. So they stay home.

It's not easy to love one another, you know. It's not easy. We don't always know just how to express our affection for one another. One of the pastors in our class this week told the story of a woman in his congregation. Nancy, I think, was her name. And Nancy always worshipped in the same pew near the back of the sanctuary. One Sunday morning, Nancy came in and sat down in her pew. But a young family with a couple of children, visiting the church for the first time, came in and sat down in her pew, right beside her. And she said to them, "You can't sit there. That's Baron's pew." And they said, "Who's Baron?" And she said, "Baron's my husband." And they said, "Well, where is he?" And she said, "Well, he died a couple of months ago, but that's his pew, and you can't sit there."

Okay, are you ready for this? Rather than taking offense, this couple said to Nancy, "That must be very painful for you. Why don't you come to lunch with us after worship and tell us about Baron?" And they stayed in the pew and took her to lunch. And then in the weeks that followed, they called her, and they visited her, and they invited her to do things with their family.

After about a year had passed, Nancy shared this story with her pastor, confessing that she regretted her initial attitude. "You know," she told her pastor, "that young family has become as close to me now as my own children are."

You never know where love is going to break out. Where love is going to happen. But it's not easy. We are no longer strangers. We don't always know one another's names. We don't always know one another's stories, but we are part of a family. A family that began there at the first supper when Jesus said, "Love one another as I have loved you."

I have one last story to tell you about my week and then we'll close. Our workshop leader was a pastor who is currently serving a congregation in Toledo, Ohio. He traveled to Pittsburgh to teach the class. During one of our breaks, I struck up a conversation with him and asked him about his family. He said he had grown children in various places around the country. He said, "I have a son who lives in Lake Alfred, Florida." And I said, "Lake Alfred! I'm from Winter Haven, ten miles down the road from Lake Alfred. Small world." So later on that week, he saw me again and he said he had just talked to his son in Lake Alfred. And he went on to share with me that his son's wife, 36 years old, had that very day, had cancer surgery in Winter Haven.

I thought to myself, "He's come from Toledo, Ohio. I've come from Winter Haven, Florida. Here we are together in Pittsburgh, Pennsylvania. Meanwhile, his daughter-in-law is having what was very successful surgery in Winter Haven, and members of my congregation there are very probably caring for his daughter-in-law in the hospital as she convalesces." Some of you here this morning may know her as a friend. Some of your kids may play soccer with her kids. Some of you may work in the same office where she works.
We are no longer strangers. We belong to one family. And it's not always easy to love one another. It's not always easy. Often it takes patience. And courage. And sometimes, stubborn persistence. That's why God wants you on the team.

Let us pray:

Loving God, open our hearts and our spirits to welcome and to be welcomed. In Jesus Christ, Amen.

Filioque

Because you are sons and daughters, God has sent the spirit of his Son into our hearts, crying, "Abba! Father!" Galatians 4: 6

Have you ever been to a Greek wedding? Maybe you saw the movie. If you have ever been to a Greek Orthodox wedding or worshipped in a Greek Orthodox sanctuary, you know that it is a little different than the way we do things here in a Presbyterian church. Very elaborate vestments for the priest. Colorful rituals. They have a lot more candles than we do. And incense. I don't know why we couldn't have incense once in a while. There is no theological reason we couldn't have incense. I think we should have an incense Sunday. Anybody with me?

The Orthodox family of churches – Greek, Russian, Romanian, and others -- all have a shared heritage. We refer to them as the Christian Churches of the East because they have their roots on the eastern edge of the Mediterranean and trace their heritage to Constantinople (now Istanbul, Turkey). What we call the Western churches are those churches that trace their history more through Rome, including of course the Roman Catholic Church, but also the Protestant churches in what was thought of as the "Western" part of the world. So we are one of the Western Churches.

None of this mattered to a soul until the year 1054. In 1054 the one Christian Church extending across most of Europe broke apart, divided by controversy. They divorced. And it wasn't a happy divorce. There was bitterness. And even violence. The church split right down the middle. And it did so for reasons that had to do with the personalities of the people who were in leadership at that time; and it had to do with politics; and it had to do with geography and differences in language. But it also had to do with a fundamental difference in what they believed. A theological difference. And that theological difference was captured in one disputed word. It is an exaggeration to say that one word divided the church, but it is not much of an exaggeration.

And that one word which split the church a thousand years ago is the word *Filioque*. *Filioque* (fill-ee-o-quay). One side believed that the doctrine expressed in the word *Filioque* was not only true but essential to Christian faith. The other side believed that the doctrine expressed in the word *Filioque* is not only false but insisted that if you failed to recognize that it is false, you couldn't be a part of the true church.

So where do you stand? Raise your hand if you think *Filioque* is true? You can guess if you want. Who thinks *Filioque* was true? Oh my goodness! Who thinks *Filioque* was false? You are reluctant to vote; I don't blame you. Do you want to know what you are voting on?

Both sides believed that there is one God. Both sides believed that the one God exists as Father, Son, and Holy Spirit; we call that the Trinity. Both sides affirmed the Trinity. Both sides said, "Jesus Christ is the son of God". They both agreed on that. Both sides said, "Jesus Christ is the *begotten* son of God." That's the word they used, begotten, to describe the relationship between the Father and the Son. The Son is begotten of the Father. Both sides believed it. And both sides believed in the Holy Spirit.

But what do you say about the relationship between the Holy Spirit and the Father. And the Son? If you say the Holy Spirit is *begotten* just the same as the Son, if you say the same word, then logically that makes the Holy Spirit and Jesus *brothers*! And that didn't sound right. And in some languages the words for Holy Spirit are feminine in gender, so if you say the Holy Spirit is begotten, then Jesus and the Holy Spirit are brother and sister!

So they had to come up with another way to describe this relationship. The Church decided on the words *proceeds from*. The Holy Spirit proceeds from the Father. (Aren't you glad you're here this morning?) And both sides agreed on that. The Holy Spirit proceeds from the Father. But the Western Church added one word: *Filioque*. They said, "The Holy Spirit proceeds from the Father *and from the Son*." *Filioque* means "and from the Son." And the Western Church wanted to say that if you have the Holy Spirit proceeding only from the Father, then that leaves the Son of God out of it. He's diminished, demoted so to speak. He's out of the action. So you have to include the Son. The Western Church argued that the Holy Spirit proceeds from the Father and from the Son. *Filioque*.

And the Eastern Church said, "No. That's wrong. The Holy Spirit proceeds only from the Father." And that was basically the argument that divided the church in 1054. And the separation that resulted from that argument exists today. We're still divided. Now I do not believe that the church must be organizationally united in order to be faithful. I mean, I don't think we all have to get together in one big super, super bureaucracy in order to be faithful. The Methodists have their system; that's fine. The Baptists have theirs. The Presbyterians have our system; that's fine. The Roman Catholics have their system; that's fine. Orthodox Churches. Fine. I don't see too much wrong with that today.

But let me remind you, if I may, what happened in the world in the 300 years the Church spent debating this one word. From approximately 700 A.D. to the split in 1054, the Church was preoccupied and to an extent paralyzed by this squabble over *Filioque*. Do you remember what was going on? A new religious faith had arisen in the Middle East at the beginning of that 300-year period, a faith that worshipped one God and honored Abraham and Moses and Jesus as great prophets. And that new religious faith spread across the civilized world from Spain in the West to India in the East, and beyond. While Christians fussed over *Filioque*, that new religious faith was winning the hearts and minds of ordinary people all across the known world. Why is it that in the very birthplace of Christian faith, in Jordan and Palestine, in Syria and Egypt and Turkey, in those places where the Christian Church was born, Christians are today a tiny minority? In the very towns and regions where the first Christians gave their lives to tell the good news of Jesus the Savior, the overwhelming majorities of those populations belong to that new faith, the Muslim faith. And as I've said before, Muslim believers have every right to spread their faith, as do adherents of Judaism, Christianity, or whatever. And while they were sharing their faith, we Christians were fighting among ourselves. That's what happened.

Well, this went on for a couple of centuries after the split until, finally, the Church came to realize how destructive this was. And so in the year 1438, the Roman pope, Eugene IV and the spiritual leader of the Eastern Church, Patriarch Joseph II got together! They called a big meeting. The Emperor of the Holy Roman Empire was there to moderate the meeting. It was a big deal! They gathered in the city of

Florence, Italy; East and West came together to see if they couldn't work this out. Pope Eugene brought his Cardinals from the West and Joseph brought his Patriarchs and spiritual leaders from the East. And they sat down at the conference table in October of 1438. And they met all winter long. You think our committee meetings here take a long time. And on the 8th of June in the year 1439, they had a breakthrough. They had a breakthrough over the differences that divided them

Over the centuries of separation their differences had, of course, grown. The first big issue was the authority of Rome. Rome and the Western Church said, you know, that there could be only one spiritual leader of the church and that had to be the Pope in Rome. And the folks in the East said, "Well, we've got a lot of spiritual leaders ourselves over here in the East." So they worked out a compromise: the folks in the East agreed to recognize the authority of Rome; and the Pope's team agreed to recognize that spiritual leaders in the East should have a measure of authority in the East. Eugene said, "Okay." Joseph said, "Okay." And they had a deal on that.

The next issue was even more difficult. In the East, for at least four centuries, priests had been free to marry. That was the practice there; the priests could marry. And many did marry and had families, children, grandchildren. In the West, priests couldn't marry. So folks in the East said, "Hey." (I'm improvising the dialogue; this isn't verbatim, but you probably knew that. I'm relying here on Williston Walker's account of this negotiation in his classic work, *A History of the Christian Church*.) "Hey, we can't have our priests abandoning their wives and families; marriage is part of our tradition here." And Pope Eugene in the West said essentially, "Well, the idea of a married clergy doesn't seem like a very good idea, but we can live with it. We'll go ahead and recognize your priests, and permit priests to marry on a limited basis."

Did you know they worked that out? So that left the last and most difficult issue, *Filioque*. And the East took the lead on that. They said, "Ok, you're making a good argument here. We're not trying to diminish the Son. Maybe we can work out a deal. Suppose that we say that we recognize that the Holy Spirit proceeded from the Father *through* the Son?" And Pope Eugene said, "Well, that's not exactly what we mean, but it is close. We can live with that." And Joseph said, "Alright, we will affirm the doctrine of *Filioque* if you don't make us say it every Sunday in worship." And Pope Eugene said, "Deal." So they shook hands or whatever Patriarchs and Popes do when they make a deal. They probably embraced one another and kissed one another, then went outside and issued a statement saying, "We fixed it! The church is reunited!"

Did you know that? Did you know that on June 10th in the year 1439 the Western branch of Christianity and the Eastern branch of Christianity agreed to put aside their differences and reunite Christ's Church? Chances are you didn't know that, and for a very good reason.

Two days after the deal was made, Patriarch Joseph II died. He never made it back to Constantinople to sell and seal the deal. No one else in the Eastern delegation had the moral authority and influence of the beloved Patriarch Joseph. So the deal fell apart.

They waited too long to fix it! In the preceding 400 years the bitterness had grown too deep. The distrust and suspicion had grown too strong. Think about how different the history of the Christian Church might have been if they had gotten together and solved it six months earlier, or a year earlier. Think how different the history of Christianity, or for that matter, the history of the whole world might have been if the Church had been united for this past millennia, rather than divided.

Maybe that is the point of this whole sad story of the doctrine of *Filioque*. Maybe the point is that if something is broken, especially a relationship, don't wait 400 years to fix it. Fix it while you can.

Well, representatives of the Eastern and Western Churches sat down together again in the year 2002. They had been getting together every decade or so for years, but in 2002, they made some progress. They didn't get as far as they had gotten 550 years ago, but they made some progress. They issued a joint statement addressing the theological questions raised by the doctrine of *Filioque*. I'm going to paraphrase their first point for you. (This isn't exactly what they said because they put it in "church" language; they didn't say it quite as bluntly as I'm going to say it.) But this is what I think they meant in their joint statement: persons who undertake to describe in human words the inner life of the holy God is on a fool's errand. We simply don't have human words to describe the mystery of God's inner life.

Often, on Sundays when the Lord's Supper is served, we sing the marvelous Communion hymn, "You Satisfy the Hungry Heart." We sing, "The mystery of your presence Lord, No human tongue can tell: Whom all the world cannot contain, Comes into our hearts to dwell." That's the message of Pentecost Sunday. The holy mystery of God dwells within us.

Let us pray.

Freely we confess, O God, that we have often squabbled over trivial things while missing the heart of your call to us; so renew us and fill us again with your Spirit. In Jesus Christ Amen.

The History Of Halloween

When the perishable puts on the imperishable, when the mortal puts on immortality, then shall come to pass the saying that is written: "Death is swallowed up in victory. O Death, where is thy victory? O Death, where is thy sting?" The sting of death is sin and the power of sin is the law. But thanks be to God who gives us the victory through our Lord Jesus Christ. Therefore, my beloved brothers and sisters, be steadfast, immovable, always abounding in the work of the Lord, knowing that in the Lord your labor is not in vain. I Corinthians 15: 54-58

It's been a busy week here at the church. Busy week at home, too. The telephone has just not stopped ringing at home. If I told you who called me this week, you wouldn't believe me! Some of the most important people in the country have called me this week and asked for my help; I guess there's an election next week.

When I was serving a parish in Ohio a few years ago, there was a dust-up in our community, a little controversy about Halloween. It began with some very conservative pastors protesting the celebration of Halloween in our community. They said it is a celebration of the occult and a glorification of Satanism and witchcraft. They appealed to the school board; principals received angry letters. Parents threatened to withhold their children from school if Halloween celebrations were not canceled. And they pointed out that the Puritans, the Pilgrims, didn't celebrate Halloween. Of course, they didn't celebrate Christmas either. The controversy lasted a couple of years; I don't know whether it got down here to Florida or to the communities where you live. Anybody remember the Halloween controversy from a few years ago?

It didn't last very long because that dust-up gave us the opportunity to remember our history and the history of Halloween. The holiday we know as Halloween used to be called *Allhalloweven*. But that was too hard to say, so they dropped the *v* out of it. But it's All Hallows' Eve. We remember that All Hallows' Eve affirms one of the great truths of Christian faith. And that's what I want to talk to you about this morning.

Aren't You Glad You're Here This Morning?

Did you know that the origins of our observance of Halloween are older than Christmas? Older even than Easter. The Celts in Great Britain and Northern Europe observed a day like Halloween more than two thousand years ago. They were instructed by a clan called the Druids – you've heard of the Druids, Stonehenge, and all that. And on the last day of October they worshipped a god with the awkward name of Samhain, probably a Scottish name. Samhain was the lord of death. And the 31rst of October was his day. Because with the onset of autumn and the growing darkness of the season, winter was coming in the Northern Hemisphere. The leaves were dying and the crops were perishing. It was the season of darkness and death. And followers of Samhain believed that November 1st was the first day of the New Year. Their new year began in darkness on November 1st. So October 31st was really a kind of New Year's Eve observance, though not with joy and not with celebration.

Now just an interesting side light, I think: if you count the months in the Roman calendar – you know, the Roman calendar begins with March, a ten-month calendar. March, April, May, June etc. September is the 7th month (*sept* is seven), October is the 8th month (*oct* is eight), November is the 9th month (*nova* is nine), and December the 10th month (*deca*, you know, ten). But an interesting thing happened. Even though the Celts were living under the Roman calendar two thousand years ago, they didn't pay any attention to the Roman calendar. They stayed with their own traditions and celebrated the New Year, the beginning of the year on November 1st. So that prefix *Nova* in November, which was the Latin *nine*, came also to mean *new*. And it goes back to the Celts. If you have an idea that is new, somebody may describe it as "novel." It doesn't mean it's the ninth idea, it means it's new. We may travel to *Nova* Scotia – New Scotland. That word "nova" came to mean something new. It's clear in Spanish, which comes from Latin origins. The number nine in Spanish is *nueve*; the word for new in Spanish is *nuevo*, new. It all goes back to the Celts. Aren't you glad you're here this morning? You learned all this. And so the ninth month came to mean the new year. And on the last day of the old year, October 31, Samhain released the prisoners held by death.

He opened the doors of death's prison, they believed. For one night, the spirits were released to roam the earth. That is the origin of our

Halloween celebration. The spirits would be released, both good and evil. And the evil spirits would come threatening. So to protect themselves against the evil spirits, people began in those days to wear disguises. Masks. They began to dress themselves like skeletons or witches or gremlins or evil spirits so that the evil spirits who came out that night wouldn't recognize them, would think they were part of the team. And that's why we costume at Halloween. To hide from the evil spirits. And that's how they got to carving pumpkins too. Carve this little light, a smiling face, or a frowning face, to scare away the evil spirits. But did you know that pumpkins are an American fruit – or are they a vegetable? They're American. In Europe they carved – anybody know this, what they carved? Turnips! Turnips. Think about that! You think a pumpkin is hard to carve? Turnips. Find a big turnip, hollow it out, carve a face, and set it in the window with a candle to scare away the evil spirits.

This was the origin of Halloween. What happened was that even after the people of Britain and Northern Europe came to Christian faith, they still observed the old cultural customs, they still observed Halloween. And so about 800 AD, during the reign of Charlemagne – anybody remember Charlemagne from your high school history classes? During the reign of Charlemagne, the church said to itself (and I'm oversimplifying this a little bit) the church said, "Look, if people are going to celebrate this pagan holiday on October 31st, if they're going to observe the lord of death, if they're going to have a party anyway, let's give them something to celebrate that affirms our faith." And so the church said, "Let's set November 1st as All Saints' Day, the day we remember those who have gone before us, our loved ones who have died and passed on to heaven." The church said, "Let's celebrate that on November 1st. Instead of celebrating the lord of death, Samhain, let's celebrate the Lord of Life. Instead of celebrating that our loved ones are released from death's hold one night of the year, let's celebrate that by the victory of Jesus Christ, they are released to life in eternity with God and with the loved ones who have gone before them."

And so, All Hallows' Eve became not a night of dread, not a night of fear, but a night to celebrate the victory of God, and to remember the loved ones who had gone before. I'll bet you've never heard this before. In a very real sense, Halloween is the second Easter of the year! On Easter morning, we celebrate the fact that death could not hold Christ. He arose from the grave. On Halloween we celebrate the fact that death cannot hold our loved ones, that they are released from the power of death in the victory of Jesus Christ. Death does not get the last word; life gets the last word. God gets the last word.

Now, the costumes that we wear on Halloween have a very different meaning. Go ahead, wear your skeleton costume, dress up as a witch or an evil spirit. Go ahead. Because it has a very different meaning now. We're not doing that now because we're afraid. We're doing that to show a holy mockery of our old enemy, Death. We win. He doesn't. So dress up and mock him. Happy Halloween!

The church adopted this pagan holiday and gave it a whole new meaning. If you've been in Presbyterian churches very often on the last Sunday of October, you know that this is the day we call Reformation Sunday. That's why we sang Martin Luther's great hymn today. It's the day on which Martin Luther nailed his document to the door of the Wittenburg Chapel. We celebrate that event on this day. Do you know why Luther did that on the 31st of October? Because it was Halloween! That's why he chose that day to begin to reform the church, because it was this great day of resurrection and promise and hope. It's no accident that Reformation Sunday falls on All Hallows' Eve. Luther intended it that way. The great hymn which we just sang: *"The prince of darkness grim, we tremble not for him, his reign we can endure. For lo, his doom is sure. One little word shall fell him."* That's our Halloween Anthem. It's All Hallows' Eve; rejoice in the victory of God.

Now there's one more detail about the calendar that I should point out to you before we close. The New Year for the Celts, November 1st, marked the coming of darkness. The coming of death. But if you're carefully watching the sky, if you're carefully observing the seasons, the days are shortening a lot on November 1st and 2nd and 3rd. But what is the first day of the calendar when the light stops receding? When is the first day of the calendar when the light begins to return? It falls on our calendar between the 22nd and 23rd of December. In that 24-hour period the light stops receding. On the 23rd it begins to return and if you take a day to plan the party and get the word out to the rest of the village, then the day to celebrate the return of the light is December 25th. Christmas. Halloween and Christmas are related, you see. The departure of the light and the return of the light. Did you know this? What a great holiday this is!

Frederick Buechner remembers those saints who have been important in his life -- mother, father, brothers, sisters, grandparents -- and this is his meditation for All Saints Day:

"How they do live on, those giants of our childhood. And how well they manage to take even death in their stride. Because death can never put an end to our relationship with them. Wherever or however else they may have come to life since, it is beyond a doubt that they live still in us." And he concludes, "I could not imagine who I would have been without them."

That is what we celebrate on this weekend. St. Paul said, "Death, where is your victory? Where is your sting? We have won the victory in Jesus Christ." So Happy Halloween. Happy Easter. Happy All Hallows' Eve.

Let us pray:

Loving God, we thank you for all of those loved ones whose faces and voices and love we do now remember with gratitude, wonder, and deep joy. In Jesus Christ, Amen.

Walking On Water

Immediately, Jesus made his disciples get into the boat and go before him to the other side, to Bethsaida, while he dismissed the crowd. And after he had taken leave of them, he went up on the mountain to pray. Now when evening came, the boat was out on the sea, and he was alone on the land. And he saw that they were making headway painfully, for the wind was against them. And about the fourth watch of the night, he came to them walking on the sea. He meant to pass by them, but when they saw him walking on the sea, they thought it was a ghost and cried out, for they all saw him and were terrified. But immediately he spoke to them and said "Take heart, it is I. Have no fear." And he got into the boat with them, and the wind ceased.
Mark 6: 45-51

Why doesn't everybody believe?

The church has asked that question for centuries. Why doesn't everybody believe, why aren't the pews completely filled this morning and every Sunday morning? Why doesn't everybody believe? *We* are here this morning because it makes sense to us, you know. We've heard the stories, and we may have doubts and questions, but we believe enough to be here. Why doesn't everybody? It's not that we're smarter than they are. Well, you may be smarter, but it's not a matter of intelligence. Why do some people believe, and other people just don't believe at all?

The church has often answered that question by saying it's a matter of "hardness of heart". Their hearts are hardened; that's why they don't believe. I'm not at all satisfied with that answer, because I know that sometimes my heart is as hard as any human heart could be. And maybe your heart gets hard too sometimes. Yet we still believe. So I don't believe hardness of heart explains it. I think there's a better explanation.

Most of us, when we hear these stories or read them, place them in one of two categories. We read along through the story and say to ourselves, "That's possible; that's possible; that's possible; oops, that's impossible." And we put the "impossible" stuff in a different category. Doesn't mean you *don't* believe it. You can believe impossible things. Many people do. And indeed that's what some critics of the church say: "Church people believe impossible things."

So let's see how it works. Let's take the story of the feeding of the 5,000 for example. You know that story. Jesus gathered 5,000 people on a hillside: that's possible. And he taught them concerning the Kingdom of God; that's possible. And they got hungry; that's possible. And the disciples found a little boy that had five loaves and two fish: that's possible. And Jesus took the five loaves and two fish and gave thanks to God: that's possible. And then he broke it up and passed it out to the crowd and they all ate and were satisfied; then they gathered up twelve basketsful of leftovers; that's impossible! So: possible, possible, possible, impossible. Put the impossible over there in the impossible bucket. We do it unconsciously. You can still choose to believe what's in the impossible bucket if you want to, but that is the problem for many people. They're not willing to believe what everybody knows is impossible.

So maybe what we need to do as modern progressive-thinking Christians is to put the impossible things in a bucket and set them aside. Concentrate on the parts of religion that are reasonably possible. That's what Thomas Jefferson did. Remember the third President of the United States, Thomas Jefferson? He pieced together his own version of the Bible. He kept the things that were possible and excluded the things that he thought were impossible. Did you know that? When people say, "We need to get back to the faith of our Founding Fathers" -- well, that was Jefferson's faith. He was a deeply religious man. Deeply religious man. You can probably find his version on the Internet. Just click on the Jefferson Bible, and there it'll be. Jefferson relied on *reason* to decide what was possible, then excluded everything that was *not* reasonably possible. And if that's what you feel you need to do, then do it. But let me give you a word of caution.

The difference between what's possible and what's impossible is not always precisely clear. In every religion that I know of, between what's possible and what's impossible, there is a little gap, a *space*. And that space we call *mystery*. Or *wonder*. Every religion has it. And sooner or later on your journey of faith, you have to go through that space to get anywhere. Depending on who you are and what your life experiences have been, the space may be larger or smaller. But there will always be some space between how far reason can take you and where faith invites you to go. Mystery fills that space. Reason can take you a long way, all the way up to the edge of that space. Even if your belief system is pure science and you believe only what is scientifically verifiable, there is still a gap there, a space. Even science has its mystery. What happens when science runs up against a reality that no one can yet satisfactorily explain, a mystery? Someone postulates a working *theory* to bridge the gap, and the work goes forward.

Maybe you have tried this with your kids. Suppose that you decide to walk home from church today. The rain has ended, I think. Leave your car here; we can use it. Walk home today. In the first hour after church, walk halfway home. Then sit down somewhere safe and rest. In the second hour after church, walk half of the rest of the way home, sit down and rest. And then in the third hour after church, walk half of whatever you have left to get to your house, then rest again if you need to. You might be getting a little hungry by then, or at least thirsty, so I hope you take along some refreshment. If you continue your journey home by stopping for a rest halfway into the remaining distance, what time will you get home?

Never? Right! I guess you've tried this. Maybe some of you are here resting right now, halfway to somewhere else! You'll never get home. There will always be half a space. It may be only an inch or two; don't cheat. Now we all know that this is absurd, but theoretically, you'll never get home if you only go halfway at a time.

That's how faith works! Reason alone, as important as it is, can never take you all the way home. At some point, you've got to cross that space of mystery and wonder. You have to take the whole step, you know, and cross that space to get home to faith.

Well, that's the caution. You can remove from your faith the things that are impossible but be careful because it's not always clear. Consider this story that is our subject this morning, Jesus walking on water. Jesus was out in the hills, teaching his disciples; that's possible.

He put them in a boat and sent them out upon the sea; that's possible. They were rowing hard, the wind was against them, and they weren't making much headway; that's possible. So Jesus, still up on the land, saw them even though it was night. Maybe the lighting flashed, or moonlight, or whatever; that's possible. And then he walked out across the sea to meet them; that's impossible. Right?

Well, did you ever see someone water skiing?

"That's different!" you say. "Water skiing isn't walking on water. Skiers have those big boards on their feet to keep them afloat."

Well, have you ever seen barefoot skiing?

"That's not the same, that's different," you answer. "That involves speed."

All right then, have you ever been to a pond to see a water skipper? Ever have a lizard in your pool? They don't have water skis, and there they are walking across the surface of the water.

"Oh," you say, "That's different. That doesn't count. That doesn't prove anything."

Well, of course it doesn't *prove* anything. But can you walk on water? Come with me up to the shores of Lake Erie this January morning, and I will walk you halfway to Canada.

Can you walk on water? Well, you know, it all depends. So the line between what's possible and what's impossible isn't always as clear as we might think it is.

Peter Gomes, former chaplain at Harvard University, explained the difference between magic and mystery. Magic asks the question, "How did he do that?" Mystery asks the question, "What does it mean?" In this story about Jesus walking on water, the right question is not, "How did he do that?" The question to ask is, "What does it mean?"

Magic asks, "How did he do that?" Now, I'm probably going to regret this, but everybody knows it's impossible to pull a white handkerchief out of an empty hat, right? Right? Is this hat empty? Empty, thank you. The hat is empty, and everybody knows it's impossible to pull a handkerchief out of an empty hat.

So let's just try this here. Say the magic words for me. And here is the white handkerchief! Magic asks, "How did he do that?" (That's my only magic trick. I won't blame you if you never come back to this church again).

Mystery asks, "What does it mean?" What does it mean that Jesus left his prayers in the mountains to help his friends? When the disciples got into a fix, when they got into trouble, he came to them walking on the sea. What does it mean?

For the Jews, the sea was always a dangerous and foreboding place. They were the people of the land; even the fisherman weren't comfortable on the sea. They carried in their collective memory the story of Noah: water is danger. Only God's mercy and forbearance keeps the chaos of the sea from overwhelming us.

So what does it mean that Jesus comes walking on *water*? This is what it meant for the author of Mark's Gospel: there is no place that Jesus won't go to help his friends. Wherever we go, wherever the journey of life may take us, there is no place so far that he is not near.

When they read this account of Jesus walking on water, many commentators suggest – and you've probably heard this before – they suggest that in the darkness and confusion of the storm, the disciples drifted closer to the shore than they realized. What they saw was Jesus walking *by* the sea, or wading in the shallow surf. If that works for you, fine. Believe as much as you can believe. But respect the integrity of those who believe a little less, or a little more, than you can.

Then Jesus said to his disciples, "Have no fear." The sea holds no terror now: he is Master of the sea. The storm is becalmed in his presence. "Have no fear," he said. He intended it as something more than a suggestion. It was a command. The people of God are called to courage. When the wind blows in your face and the storm lashes, when the tide is running against you, when the darkness descends and the sheltering harbor disappears in the gloom, you are not alone.

This is what Mark's Gospel hopes we *can* believe: when you need a friend in a storm, Jesus will stand with you, even if he has to walk on water to get there.

Let us pray:

Loving God, in the turmoil of modern life, let us know the great calm of your peace. In Jesus Christ, Amen.

When All The Old Normals Have Changed*

God is our refuge and strength, a very present help in trouble.
Therefore, we will not fear, though the earth should change,
though the mountains shake in the heart of the sea.
Though its waters roar and foam, though the mountains tremble with tumult.
There is a river whose streams make glad the city of God,
the holy habitation of the Most High.
God is in the midst of her, she shall not be moved.
God will help her, and that right early.
The nations rage, the kingdoms totter: he utters his voice and the earth melts.
The Lord of Hosts is with us; the God of Jacob is our refuge.
Be still, and know that I am God. Psalm 46

I didn't intend to begin this morning by talking about hurricanes, but there's been so much of it in the news this week. I haven't heard any mention of one part of the story that I thought might interest you. If you already know this story, good for you.

New York City is under a hurricane warning this morning. It will not be their first. In the year 1938, there were no weather satellites. There were no spotter planes. Forecasting was primitive. Three days before the storm hit New York City, it was spotted off Jacksonville. The weather forecasters in Jacksonville did the right thing. They notified people up and down the coast that there was a hurricane in the Atlantic. But it was in that triangle of ocean that has since come to be known as the Bermuda Triangle, so no one was particularly anxious to head out there to investigate. After the storm passed Jacksonville, it disappeared for a while. Then it clipped Cape Hatteras, just as Irene has done. Then the storm turned out to sea again and disappeared.

The weather forecast for September 21st, 1938, in New York City was cooler and rainy. At 2:00 in the afternoon on the 21st, a forty-foot-high wall of water hit Long Island. At one point, Long Island itself was cut in two by the rising tide. It hit New York City as it will do today, just at high tide. There are no exact numbers, but it was estimated that the hurricane was rotating at 200 miles an hour when it made landfall. In today's terms, that would make it a Category 4 storm. More than 700 people died, making it the deadliest hurricane in American history until Katrina. But if I had asked you where the most devastating and deadly hurricane had hit, who would have said New York City? You might have said Galveston or Mobile or Jacksonville or Charleston. But who would have named New York City? Don't feel bad if you didn't know that.

On September 21st, 1938, the most devastating hurricane in American history wasn't even front-page news in most cities. There was something else going on in the world that day, and in the days that followed. In Europe, Adolf Hitler was on the march. And on the 21st of September, German forces occupied the nation of Czechoslovakia. And most everyone understood that this was the prelude to a world war.

In normal times, the most devastating hurricane in history would have been a headline, but those were not normal times. We are not the first generation to live in a world of tumultuous change, when all the old normals seem to have come undone.

What's the first thing you say after some interruption to your life, an illness, an accident, a storm? "Oh, if we could only get back to normal! When will we get back to normal?" What I'm talking about this morning is not primarily the wider world of global change. Oh there is plenty of change to talk about on the world stage. But I'd like to focus for a moment on a more personal variety of change.

When you bring a new baby into the house, all the old normals change. When you give up your home, and make that move into a retirement community, all the old normals will change. When you care for a loved one at home who is recovering from surgery or recovering from some long illness, and your living room becomes a hospital room, all the old normals change. When your first child goes to school or your last child goes to college or to the military service, all the old normals have changed. And certainly the death of a spouse means that for a long time, all of the old comfortable normals must change.

The psalmist said, "God is our refuge. We will not fear, though the earth should change." I wish I could climb up to that high ground! Don't you wish we could all face change without anxiety, without fear? I wish I could. I'm not there yet. "We will not fear, though the earth should change." If I have to choose between a worn-out normal and God's promise of help in tumultuous change, I'll take the worn-out normal any day. How about you?

Somebody said to me this week -- and you have to think about this a minute; I had to think about this before I got it – somebody said to me this week, "You can't be argued out of something that you weren't argued into." In other words, if you have a belief or an opinion or an attitude about something, you can't be argued out of it if you didn't get into it by being argued into it. Please remember that sentence when you attend your next committee meeting. You can't be argued out of something that you weren't argued into. Think about it. Most of us change our attitudes or opinions about things *not* because we've heard a more rational argument, *not* because we've heard a better idea, but because we *have to* change. We change when we have no choice. We change when we must change.

For a long time when I was younger, my breakfast menu consisted of two cups of coffee and two donuts. Wherever I was, home or out someplace, that's what I'd order. That's what I'd have. Two cups of coffee and two donuts, and that was my breakfast. College, the first church I served, far into my adult years. Twenties, thirties – I did that, it didn't hurt me any. I've learned since that so many donuts may cause your hair to fall out.

Now people at the time said, "That's not a very nourishing breakfast for you. You should eat something more nourishing. Breakfast is the most important meal of the day." Most important meal of the day; that didn't faze me at all. I kept having my two cups of coffee and two donuts. But then when I got into my forties, my metabolism began to change. My metabolism changed, and by 11:00, if I had eaten only two cups of coffee and two donuts, I'd begin to get weak. You know, you get hungry and weak. The caffeine takes you up, and the sugar goes up, and then it comes down, you know, and you begin to crash. And by 11:30 when I'd had two cups of coffee and two donuts for breakfast, by 11:30 my hands were shaking so bad that I could barely hold the steering wheel to drive myself down to KFC for a more nourishing lunch of fried chicken and mashed potatoes. So I had to change, you know. I didn't want to change. And I didn't change my breakfast menu because somebody had argued me into eating a healthier breakfast.

The psalmist said, "We will not fear though the earth change," and I wish I could climb up to that high ground. But he said something even more difficult than that, or maybe more wonderful than that. The psalmist also said, "There is a river whose streams make glad" – well, let's just stop there – "There is a river whose streams make glad." In the midst of tumultuous change, when all the old normals are coming apart, there is, nevertheless, a river of gladness. When you find it, you can drink from it, you can wade into it, even when things have gone crazy, or especially when things have gone crazy. There is a river of gladness running through the ever-shifting landscape of change, bringing the possibility that something good and glad can be found.

It's an amazing idea, isn't it? Even when we have to give up all the normal comfortable things we love and cherish, even when we have to change, there can still be hidden within that change the possibility of gladness. Gladness.

I want to close this morning by telling you about a film that I saw this week. I should have gone to bed, but I watched the news and then I was surfing the channels and I stumbled upon this old film. And what caught my eye at first was that Hal Holbrook was the star. Who knows Hal Holbrook the actor? He's done great work. He was the star of this movie, *That Evening Sun*. That Evening Sun, like sunshine. Anybody ever see the movie? Okay. Anybody else?

Don't see the movie. It is depressing. It is just so depressing. I watched the movie for you, and now I'm going to tell you about it, so you don't have to see it. The only reason you would want to watch this movie is if you've been troubled lately by delirious happiness, and you need something to bring you back down to earth.

The movie is about Abner Meacham, who's an old man now. That's Hal Holbrook's character. And Abner has just escaped from a retirement home. He's checked himself out of a retirement home that his son checked him into three months before. And Abner said, "I was lonelier in that home surrounded by people than I ever was by myself on my farm." And so Abner checks out of the retirement home, calls a taxi, and has the taxi take him 20 miles out into the countryside, the hills of Tennessee, out to his beloved farm. And he pays the taxi and it disappears down the dusty road. And Abner is home at last.

And to his horror, he discovers that his beloved farmhouse is occupied. Not by strangers, but by his archenemies for many generations, the Choat family. And he discovers that his son, the same son that put him in the nursing home, has leased his farm to the Choats. Abner is determined to break the lease and get his farm back. That worthless Lonzo Choat is sleeping in his bed, eating at his dining room table, listening to his records – it's just terrible! Abner is determined he's going to do whatever it takes to get the Choats out of the house.

There's a tenant shack on the property. There is such bitterness between them that Lonzo won't even let Abner into his own house. So Abner takes up residence in this old tenant shack. And he makes himself a bed there; that's where he's going to stay until he can get his house back.

We discover some things as the story unfolds. We discover that the previous winter Abner had come out on his front porch late one night, slipped on the ice, fell, and broke his hip. He was there on the front porch in subfreezing weather all night long. He would have died if his neighbor hadn't by chance come along and rescued him early the next morning. So we get a little bit more insight into Abner's situation, and why his son wanted to have him in a retirement home.

We also learn a little bit about Lonzo Choat, who seems like a worthless fellow. But we learn that a couple of years before, he'd been the victim of an accident at work. A forklift driver had dumped a load of lumber on Lonzo, broke both of his legs, hurt him badly. He was unable to work and provide for his family. We learn that Lonzo has leased this farm because he's tired of doing nothing and wants to make something of himself. He doesn't know a thing about farming, but he's going to give it a try. He wants to provide for his wife and for their 16-year-old daughter, who's there with him on the farm. We gain a little insight into Lonzo.

The daughter is sixteen, struggling to grow up in difficult circumstances. She is estranged, more or less, from her father Lonzo. Soon we see the daughter bring Abner a glass of iced tea on a hot day, and a plate of food. There are possibilities here. Do you see the possibilities? She needs a grandfather. She needs a grandfather and Abner needs someone to care about besides himself. There are possibilities here.

And Abner can't handle the farm anymore. He's old and too weak to do the work, but he still *knows how* to manage a farm. Lonzo is young and stronger now. He could do the work, but he doesn't *know how* to go about it. Do you see the possibilities?

I said to myself about halfway through the film, "I see what's going on here." Do you see it? The daughter is going to bridge the hostility that was between them, and Abner is going to soften. He's going to change a little bit. He's going to recognize that Lonzo could keep his beloved farm going. Lonzo is going to change a little bit. He's going to realize that his old enemy Abner Meacham could help him make something of himself, could teach him how to work the farm. Together they could save the farm and turn it into a productive situation for both families. I could see the possibilities. You see them too, don't you?

I'm going to tell you how the film ends. I'm going to tell you because I've already told you not to see it, so this is not going to ruin it for you. In the last scene of the film we see Abner Meacham standing alone in front of an empty farmhouse. The Choats are gone. Abner's son is nowhere to be seen. The farm is growing up in weeds, the fields overgrown. And there is Abner. Alone. It's very sad. They couldn't do it.

They couldn't overcome the stupid little differences that kept them apart. They might have. They could have. There was a river of gladness running there, but they couldn't get to it. They just couldn't get to it.

They couldn't change, so they lost the opportunity to drink from that river of gladness. It was there. You saw it too.

The psalmist said, "There is a river of gladness." It's worth looking for. It's worth searching for. It's there, even when all your old normals are changing.

Let us pray:

Loving God, In these times of tumult and change, be near to us and sustain us with your gifts of gladness and courage. In Jesus Christ, Amen.

*The words of the title are taken from a conversation with my father. Toward the end of their seventy-two years together, as my mother's health declined, he became her primary caregiver, a role he fulfilled with exquisite tenderness and heroic devotion. "How are you doing?" I asked one day. "All the old normals have changed," he said.

Christmas Eve

It was Christmas Eve. As was our custom we had welcomed the congregation to the manse that evening for informal worship and cookies. The last of our guests were pulling out of the driveway. It had just begun to snow. As we folded up chairs and gathered the leftover cookies, the telephone rang.

I recognized the voice of a young mother from the church who had given birth to twins earlier that week; they were dangerously premature. She was calling from the hospital. "The twins are not doing well," she said. "The doctors don't know if…sorry to call…Christmas Eve…we are afraid…could you…would you…is there any way you could come and baptize our twins? Tonight."

As you probably know, for Presbyterians, baptism must be approved at a duly called meeting of the Session. An elder must be present and baptism administered in a public worship service. There was only one answer I could give her. I said, "I'm leaving now."

Close to midnight, I stood with those parents in the Neonatal Intensive Care Unit.

We secured a cup of holy water from the drinking fountain in that holy hospital corridor. We gave thanks for the births of their daughter and son, and for God's presence with them there. With moistened fingertips I placed my hands on those two incubators and, on behalf of the whole church, spoke the ancient words.

"Children of the covenant, I baptize you…"

It was Christmas Day.

Many years later my wife and I were back in that community. My wife went into the bank to cash a check. Reading her name on the check, the young woman behind the counter asked, "Is your husband a pastor?"

"Yes, he is."

"Well then, he baptized my brother and I in the hospital on Christmas Eve."

She remembered her baptism. Or more precisely, her parents remembered and shared the story with her and her brother, perhaps each Christmas Eve.

How did Matthew and Luke know about the shepherds and the Kings, the innkeeper's manger, the angels' song, the guiding star?

Luke 2:51 tells us: "Mary kept all these things and pondered them in her heart." She remembered. And shared the story.

Now it is time to remember and share the story again. On that first Christmas Day, the whole creation is christened. Now we belong to the family of God. One family, free of the fabricated barriers of race, class, or gender, full of grace, fashioned toward compassion, and fitted for joy.

Merry Christmas

About the Author

Thomas E. McGrath is a native of New Castle, Pennsylvania. He graduated from Westminster College (Pa.). He attended Dubuque Theological Seminary and graduated from Pittsburgh Theological Seminary. He was ordained to the Ministry of Word and Sacrament by the Presbyterian Church (U.S.A.) in 1973. He earned the Doctor of Ministry degree from Columbia Theological Seminary in 1996, with a focus on gender oppression in Old Testament texts.

Dr. McGrath served Presbyterian churches in Leesburg, Pennsylvania, Ashland, Ohio, and Winter Haven, Florida. He is an Honorably Retired member of the Presbytery of San Francisco, where he has served on the Committee on Ministry. He attends the Clayton Valley Presbyterian Church, where he is an ad hoc member of the congregation's Pneumatrix Team. In his spare time, Tom is an amateur gardener, an amateur carpenter, and avid putterer.

Dr. McGrath and his wife Denise reside in Brentwood, California. She is a retired middle school math teacher. Their daughter Mari lives in Oakland and is a Senior Product and Promotion Manager for Ghirardelli Chocolate.

www.ingramcontent.com/pod-product-compliance
Lightning Source LLC
Chambersburg PA
CBHW072018110526
44592CB00012B/1364